⊕ *Martin Luther* ⊕

Martin Luther

A Brief Introduction
to His Life and Works

Paul R. Waibel
Belhaven College

Harlan Davidson, Inc.
Wheeling, Illinois 60090-6000

Visit us on the World Wide Web at www.harlandavidson.com

Library of Congress Cataloging-in-Publication Data

Waibel, Paul R.
  Martin Luther : a brief introduction to his life and works / Paul R. Waibel
    p. cm.
  ISBN 0-88295-231-5 (alk. paper)
  1. Luther, Martin, 1483–1546. I. Title.
BR325.W35 2005
284.1'092—dc22

                                    2004017440

Cover image © Pixtal/Superstock

Manufactured in the United States of America
07 06 05 04 1 2 3 MG

Contents

Foreword

The fifteenth and sixteenth centuries were a period of transition in the history of Western Civilization. Some historians have chosen to see it as the waning of the Middle Ages, while others see it as the birth of the modern world. However understood, it was an era during which the universal, yet very provincial, world of medieval Christendom was giving way to a wider world in which the individual was shaping a new world order. Like the twentieth and twenty-first centuries, during which the new world order begun in the fifteenth and sixteenth centuries gave way to the global village, it was an exciting time in which to live.

Medieval civilization was a synthesis of classical humanism and Judeo-Christianity. The Holy Roman Empire and the Roman Catholic church kept alive the classical notion of a politically and religiously unified world. The individual lived in an orderly universe created by God. Each thing God created, including the individual, was assigned a place in the great chain of being. Humans were above plants and animals but below the angels and heavenly hosts in an ascending order of purity. So too were those created as rulers above those created as workers in an agricultural economy. God, it was believed, had created some to govern, some to pray, and some to labor. The individual possessed rights, but they were the rights of the estate to which he or she belonged. A peasant or a burgher, for example, enjoyed certain rights and privileges, as well as obligations, by virtue of being a peasant or burgher. The concept of inalienable and natural rights belonging to the individual was foreign to the Middle Ages.

This very secure hierarchy of the Middle Age world in which everything had its place and function, was forever shattered in 1543 by the Polish astronomer Nicholaus Copernicus. By asserting that the sun did not revolve around the earth (the medieval model of the universe), but the reverse,

Copernicus destroyed the great-chain-of-being model, and by so doing called into question the whole social, economic, political, intellectual, and religious order. To the average person in the late Middle Ages, the world was not now as comfortable or sensible as it was before Copernicus.

Copernicus was not the only great man (or woman) of that formative period. Many great individuals walked across the stage during those two centuries leaving behind their imprint on the historical drama that is forever unfolding. Explorers and conquistadors probed the limits of the oceans and discovered and conquered civilizations previously unknown to Europeans. A new middle class of entrepreneurs and bankers developed a new economic system, later called capitalism, that liberated humankind from the biblical restraints on greed imposed by the medieval church, and made the pursuit of wealth the cardinal virtue of the modern person. A class of new monarchs, armed with their newly created wealth, brought the old feudal nobility into submission to royal authority, thus forcing feudal theory into varying degrees of conformity with the new national monarchies.

The new national monarchs of the sixteenth century sought control of the church within their territories in order to secure a strong unified nation-state. For political reasons, they desired a cooperative middle class and a submissive nobility to embrace a national church. Creation of a national church need not be achieved by shattering the unity of the medieval church, ruled over by the Roman pontiff, however. The powerful monarchs of Spain and France gained control of the Roman Catholic church, which became the national church within their territories.

For lesser would-be national monarchs, a different avenue to control of the church within their lands was provided by the Reformation, begun in 1517 by an obscure monk in the little German university town of Wittenberg. When Martin Luther brought forward his new views, he did not suffer martyrdom, the fate of the Bohemian reformer Jan Hus a century earlier, because his prince, Frederick the Wise, chose to protect him. Frederick the Wise, according to the evidence a very pious man, desired that the views Luther began to develop be given a fair hearing inside Germany. No doubt Frederick also saw in defending Luther an opportunity to further his own dynastic aspirations. A reformation in Electoral Saxony that separated the church there from the Roman Catholic church would give Frederick the Wise a national church that he could control. Many of the princes in Germany and Scandinavia were influenced by such thoughts in making their choice to support, or even introduce, the Lutheran Reformation in their lands. Almost accidentally, Martin Luther's own quest for peace with God would shatter forever the religious unity of Christendom, and at the same time hasten the growth of nation-states in Europe.

To fully appreciate Luther's role in bringing on the Reformation, it will be necessary to first introduce him by means of a brief biographical sketch in the first chapter. Then, in order to understand why Luther chose to risk his life by challenging the authority of the papacy, the reader must learn what the late medieval church taught regarding salvation. The purpose of Chapter 2 is an explanation of what Luther characterized as a "works-righteousness" approach to salvation, which will be explained later.

Luther's most important Reformation writings are considered in chronological order, beginning in Chapter 3 with the *Ninety-Five Theses*. Luther nailed the *Ninety-Five Theses* to the church door in Wittenberg on All Saints' Eve [October 31] 1517. It was meant to stimulate a debate on the issue of indulgences and in particular the selling of indulgences. That the *Ninety-Five Theses* challenged papal authority was evident to many, especially defenders of the church hierarchy. Before long, Luther was accused of heresy, and the Reformation was underway.

Chapter 4 looks at the three treatises Luther published during 1520. In these he presented what became the basic doctrines of the Protestant Reformation. In *To the Christian Nobility of the German Nation,* Luther attacked the authority of the pope, articulated his doctrine of the "priesthood of believers," and called for reform of both the church and society. In *The Babylonian Captivity of the Church,* Luther attacked the sacramental system by which the papacy exercised control over the Christian laity. Finally, in *The Freedom of a Christian,* he set forth his belief that a right understanding of how one is justified by faith (i.e., made righteous in the eyes of God) liberates the Christian from the burden and penalty of sin. Also, the Christian is liberated from the burden of attempting to earn salvation through good works in order to live a life of love and service to God and one's neighbor.

Chapter 5 examines *The Bondage of the Will,* in which Luther debated the fundamental difference between the Protestant Reformation and Christian humanism. The Protestant Reformers taught that as a result of the fall of Adam and Eve all of humanity since then bears the burden of original sin. The individual's will is so corrupted that the individual cannot, apart from God's grace, perform any good act that merits God's attention, or contributes to one's salvation. The Christian humanists believed that the individual's will was not totally corrupted by Adam and Eve's fall. They taught that by exercising reason, the individual can choose to do good works (i.e., make moral choices based upon reason) that are recognized as good by God. Therefore, the Christian humanists believed that education could produce a moral person. The Protestant Reformers denied that education alone could ever achieve such a laudable goal.

In order to provide a balanced view of Martin Luther, Chapter 6 treats his two most controversial publications, *Against the Robbing and Murdering Hordes of Peasants* (1525) and *On the Jews and Their Lies* (1543). In the former, Luther refused to support the German Peasants' Revolt of 1525. The peasants sought to rationalize their rebellion by appealing to support from Scripture and Luther's writings. But Luther asserted that rebellion against lawful authority in any form is sin and called upon the princes to suppress the rebellion, which they did brutally. The treatise is controversial because it contrasts so sharply with *The Freedom of a Christian* and other of Luther's writings. In his harsh stand against the Peasants' Revolt, Luther was defending an unjust socio-economic system.

If *Against the Robbing and Murdering Hordes of Peasants* is controversial and difficult to accept, then Luther's *On the Jews and Their Lies* is even more so. Written near the end of his life, when Luther suffered many health problems, *On the Jews and Their Lies* is a vicious anti-Semitic book that embarrassed his friends and has left a dark stain on his memory. These two works are difficult to comprehend, but necessary to include in a complete picture of Martin Luther.

Martin Luther: A Brief Introduction to His Life and Works is meant to be user friendly in several respects. The book is brief and easy to read. Each chapter ends with study aids: a summary paragraph and a short list of key events relevant to the subject of the chapter. The appendix provides an annotated list of Luther's Reformation writings available in English and published between 1955 and 1986 as *Luther's Works* (55 volumes) for those who wish to sample them to seek out a work on a particular subject. Also, a very brief Bibliographical Note will direct the reader to biographies, videos, and other resources that may serve as a starting point for a more in-depth study of this great figure in the history of the sixteenth century.

I would like to thank a number of individuals who helped with this project. The subject was suggested by Mr. Jon Farrar. Mrs. Rose Mary Foncree, Ms. Toni Lee Kraft, Dr. Joe Martin, and Dr. W. Andrew Hoffecker all read the original manuscript and made helpful suggestions. A very special thanks is due to my editor, Andrew J. Davidson, and my copy editor and production manager, Ms. Lucy Herz, whose expertise transformed my manuscript into a book. Finally, a deep debt of gratitude is owed to my wife, Darlene, and my two daughters, Elizabeth Joy and Natalie Grace, who gave me their patience and cheerful support. I offer this book with the hope that the reader will find it both informative and enjoyable.

Paul R. Waibel
Belhaven College

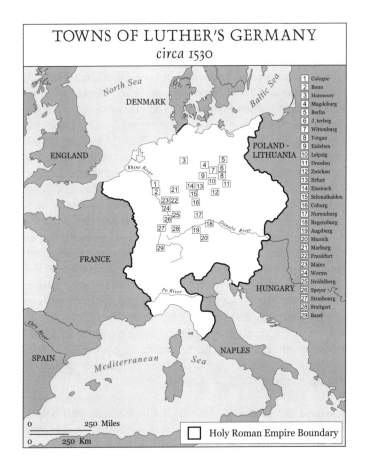

TOWNS OF LUTHER'S GERMANY
circa 1530

North Sea

Baltic Sea

DENMARK

ENGLAND

POLAND - LITHUANIA

Rhine River

FRANCE

Danube River

HUNGARY

Po River

SPAIN

Mediterranean Sea

NAPLES

1	Cologne
2	Bonn
3	Hannover
4	Magdeburg
5	Berlin
6	J terbog
7	Wittenburg
8	Torgau
9	Eisleben
10	Leipzig
11	Dresden
12	Zwickau
13	Erfurt
14	Eisenach
15	Schmalkalden
16	Coburg
17	Nuremburg
18	Regensburg
19	Augsburg
20	Munich
21	Marburg
22	Frankfurt
23	Mainz
24	Worms
25	Heidelberg
26	Speyer
27	Strasbourg
28	Stuttgart
29	Basel

0   250 Miles

0   250 Km

☐ Holy Roman Empire Boundary

⊕ CHAPTER ONE ⊕
Martin Luther, 1483–1546

In 1483, the Holy Roman Empire, or "the Empire" as it is commonly referred to by historians, was a loose confederation of more than 300 autonomous political entities, both secular and ecclesiastical. At the time of the Reformation, there was one king (the king of Bohemia), four archbishops, forty-six bishops, eighty-three other ecclesiastical lords, twenty-four secular princes, 145 counts and other secular lords, and eighty-three imperial free cities. If one includes the so-called "knights of the Empire," who acknowledged no overlord except the emperor, and who ruled over estates averaging not more than 100 acres, then the number of sovereign political entities within the Empire could reach as high as 2,000.

This crazy-quilt empire was presided over by an emperor elected since 1356 by seven electors—three ecclesiastical (the archbishops of Mainz, Trier, and Cologne) and four secular (the duke of Saxony, the margrave of Brandenburg, the count palatine of the Rhine, and the king of Bohemia). The powers of the emperor were negotiated anew at each election. In practice, the emperor's authority was limited to whatever loyalty his diverse subjects were willing to grant him.

The Holy Roman Empire was Roman in the sense that it was believed to be the successor of the Roman Empire of antiquity and thus kept alive the vision of a universal state. It was considered holy in that it was the secular counterpart of that other medieval universal empire, the Roman Catholic church, ruled over by the pope (bishop of Rome), considered to be the Successor of St. Peter and Vicar of Christ on Earth. The average German of the fifteenth century lived in the church, not the state. It was the priest with whom the

1

most individuals had almost daily contact. The church, or cathedral, if one was privileged to live within the shadow of a cathedral church, was the most important public building, and the bishop was the most important public official.

Into this world, Martin Luther was born, just before midnight on November 10, 1483, in the small town of Eisleben in Electoral Saxony. His parents, Hans and Margaretta Luther, were humble, uncultivated folk of peasant background and pious Roman Catholics. Hans Luther moved his family to Mansfeld during the year following Martin Luther's birth in hopes of improving the family's finances by pursuing a career in the copper mines. He leased a smelter from the count of Mansfeld, and soon the Luther family was enjoying the financial security of the lower middle class.

As a boy, Luther began his schooling when he was seven years old. At first he studied in the Latin School in Mansfeld; then at age twelve, he enrolled in a boarding school in Magdeburg operated by the Brethren of the Common Life, a lay (i.e., nonclerical) movement devoted to education and the promotion of a life of piety and personal communion with God. In 1498, Luther began studying at the parish school of St. George in Eisenach. On May 24, 1501, at seventeen, he enrolled at the University of Erfurt, one of the oldest and best-known universities in Germany. His father picked the university and paid the tuition. Hans Luther had great hopes for his son to become a lawyer.

Luther was a good student at the university and did his best to fulfill his father's dreams. In 1502, Martin Luther was awarded the B.A. degree and three years later, the M.A. degree. Hans proudly presented his son with a copy of the *Corpus Juris,* a compilation of Roman law made during the reign of the emperor Justinian (483–565), and made arrangements for him to begin studying law at the University of Erfurt in May 1505. It was less than two months later, on July 2, that fate intervened and altered the course of Martin Luther's life.

Luther was returning alone to the university after a visit with his parents when he was caught in a severe thunderstorm. When a bolt of lightning struck nearby, he became frightened and cried out, "Help me, St. Anne, [and] I will become a monk." To keep his vow uttered in haste, Martin Luther entered the monastery of the Augustinian Hermits in Erfurt two weeks later to the grave disappointment of his father. Within two years, he took his final vows, was ordained to the priesthood, and performed his first Mass. Although his father attended Luther's first Mass, the two were not reconciled, and Martin Luther remained troubled in his spirit by the thought of having disobeyed and disappointed his father.

When Luther entered the renowned "Black Monastery" of the Augustinian Hermits in Erfurt, he was following the path taken for centuries by numerous seekers after God. Christian monasticism dated back to the late-third and early-fourth centuries. It first appeared in the Near East and then spread to Europe during the latter fourth century. Western monasticism was given definitive form by Benedict of Nursia (c. 480–550), who founded a monastery at Monte Cassino in 529. The Rule drawn up by Benedict to regulate the daily routine of the monks became the basic rule for all Western monasteries, except those in Ireland. The monks in the monastery separated themselves from the world and its distractions, devoting themselves to a life of prayer, meditation, and study. The doors and walls of the monastery, however, never fully succeeded in shutting out the world.

By the end of the ninth century, the monasteries were no longer self-sustaining units. Often the monks, drawn from the nobility, devoted themselves to education and the liturgy, while serfs supported them with their labor. Increasingly, the monasteries became educational centers from which scholars were recruited to serve as bishops and popes or in the secular states as royal chancellors and advisers. It has been conservatively estimated that 90 percent of the literate population between 600 and 1100 were educated in monastic schools.

At various times during the Middle Ages, when the spiritual life of the institutional church (the secular, or diocesan, clergy) seemed to wane, or when the affairs of the world appeared to penetrate the protective walls of the monasteries (the regular clergy), new monastic orders arose in an attempt to recapture the original vision. The Augustinian Hermits which Luther joined was founded in the middle of the thirteenth century as a mendicant order—that is, the Augustinian monks depended upon begging for their livelihood. During the fifteenth century, the Erfurt monastery was caught up in a reform movement that had as its objective a return to strict adherence to the rule of the order. Communal meals, a rule of silence, and forsaking all private property (including books) were a part of the austere lifestyle embraced by the monks of the Black Monastery.

Although an Augustinian monk, Luther continued to study theology at the University of Erfurt. He taught at the University of Wittenberg during the winter term of 1508 and then returned to the University of Erfurt in October 1509 to press on with his theological studies. From November 1510 to April 1511, Luther and a brother monk from Erfurt journeyed to Rome on behalf of the order. What he saw there shocked him: the Roman clergy led a worldly and scandalous lifestyle unknown to monks in Germany.

Back at home, Johann von Staupitz (1460/69–1524), vicar general of the German Augustinian order, took a special interest in Luther's career. He urged Luther to pursue a doctoral degree in theology and become a teacher. Martin Luther was awarded the D.Th. degree on October 19, 1512, and soon afterwards succeeded Staupitz in the chair of biblical theology at the University of Wittenberg. In 1514, he became a priest in the parish church of Wittenberg in addition to his duties at the university, and in 1515 was appointed the Augustinian vicar for Meissen and Thuringia with responsibility for overseeing eleven monasteries. At age thirty-one, Luther was well on his way to a successful career in the church. But Luther was still a deeply troubled man. No matter how busy his many duties kept him, Luther could not find relief from his inner conflict.

Luther's problem was his inability to find peace with God. In accordance with the teachings of the church, Luther worked hard at trying to earn his salvation through good works. But no matter how hard he worked, the peace that was supposed to follow from having earned God's favor eluded him. He found only physical and emotional exhaustion. Luther said of that time, "day and night there was nothing but horror and despair." Later, in 1538, he wrote of his years as a monk:

> I was indeed a pious monk and kept the rules of my order so strictly that I can say: If ever a monk gained heaven through monkery, it should have been I. All my monastic brethren who knew me will testify to this. I would have martyred myself to death with fasting, praying, reading, and other good works had I remained a monk much longer.[1]

Sometime in the fall of 1515, Luther found the answer to his spiritual problems. He was in a tower of the monastery, studying Paul's letter to the Romans in preparation for a series of lectures on the Pauline epistles.[2] By his own account, he was pondering the meaning of Romans 1:17: "For it is the righteousness of God revealed from faith to faith; as it is written, The just shall live by faith." In that little verse Luther discovered the heart of his spiritual problem, as well as its answer.

Luther could not reconcile the two phrases in the passage from Romans, "the righteousness of God" and "The just shall live by faith." In accordance with the teaching of the medieval church and the scholastic philosophers, Luther

1 Quoted in Hans J. Hillerbrand, ed., *The Reformation: A Narrative History Related by Contemporary Observers and Participants* (Grand Rapids, MI: Baker Book House, 1978), 24.
2 Luther gave four major lecture series during the early years of his teaching career, when his theology was being formed. They were on Psalms (1513–15), Romans (1515–16), Galatians (1516–17), and Hebrews (1517–18).

understood "the righteousness of God" to refer to God as the only righteous one who judges and punishes sinners. Since all human beings are sinners from birth by virtue of original sin, and since Luther knew from his own experience that no matter how hard he tried, he could not satisfy God's standard of righteousness, Luther felt unjustly condemned by God. The belief that God set a standard for salvation that was unattainable led Luther to view God as a harsh judge, rather than a loving savior. Such a view of God left Luther feeling as though he hated the God he knew he should love. Then as Luther meditated on the phrase, "The just shall live by faith," another meaning broke through to him:

> Then, finally, God had mercy on me, and I began to understand that the righteousness of God is that gift of God by which a righteous man lives, namely, faith, and that this sentence—The righteousness of God is revealed in the Gospel—is passive, indicating that the merciful God justifies [i.e., God declares us righteous] us by faith, as it is written: 'The righteous shall live by faith.' Now I felt as though I had been reborn altogether and had entered Paradise. In the same moment the face of the whole of Scripture became apparent to me.[3]

Luther's "tower experience" has become known as one of the great moments in the history of religion. Luther's discovery in Scripture that salvation was to be achieved by grace through faith in Jesus Christ was not new, for it was the doctrine of salvation taught by the early church. Rediscovered and preached by Luther and the Protestant Reformation, the doctrine of "justification by faith" would now become the heart of the gospel as understood by Lutherans and subsequent Protestant churches. Luther believed that the individual who places his faith in Christ's self-sacrifice is freely forgiven by God. The believer's conscience is cleansed and set free from any burden of guilt for sins committed.

3 Quoted in Hillerbrand, *The Reformation,* 27.

Christians had been made to laboriously perform good works in an unsuccessful effort to gain favor with God. Now these works flowed freely from the believer who becomes an instrument of God's love, because he or she is saved by grace through faith in Jesus Christ, alone. This idea had clear ramifications: the whole human-made construct of the medieval church was no longer necessary. If salvation is a free gift of God's grace, and not a commodity dispensed by priests, then the whole clergy, from pope down to the parish priest becomes unnecessary.

Luther did not immediately begin to preach his doctrine of "justification by faith." He did not intend to challenge the church hierarchy. He was compelled to act in the fall of 1517 by his observation of the blatant abuse of the doctrine of indulgences by indulgence sellers, most notably Johann Tetzel (c. 1465–1519).[4] An indulgence was the forgiveness of all or part of the temporal punishment for sins already forgiven. The authority to forgive sins and the punishment due for them was believed to reside with the church, ultimately with the pope. From the eleventh century on, it had become standard practice for indulgences to be given on condition of contributions being made to a church or monastery. (Indulgences will be discussed further in Chapter 3.) Out of a concern for the souls of his parishioners, and wishing to call attention to the abuse of the indulgence system, Luther posted his *Ninety-Five Theses* on the church door in Wittenberg. It was meant only as an invitation to his colleagues at the university to debate the issue, but it instead triggered the Protestant Reformation.

Reformer

Initially there was very little response to the *Ninety-Five Theses,* although Luther sent copies to several bishops and friends. Members of Luther's own order, the Augustinians,

4 See Chapter 3 for a discussion of the indulgence controversy and Luther's *Ninety-Five Theses.*

debated Luther's theses in April 1518 at a meeting in Heidelberg. In December 1517, Johann Tetzel, himself a member of the Dominican order, with the help of some brother Dominican monks, prepared two sets of counter theses. Not surprisingly, it was members of the Dominican order who defended what church authorities defined as orthodoxy against the accusations embodied in Luther's *Ninety-Five Theses.* That Luther was—understandably—defended by his brother Augustinians and opposed by the Dominicans gave the appearance that this was but one more of the never ending theological disputes between rival monastic orders.

The Dominicans, or Order of Friars Preachers according to its official title, were founded in 1220 by Domingo de Guzmán (1170–1221), a cleric from Castile, who saw the need for an educated clergy capable of communicating with the people through sermons. Its original mission was to combat the Albigensian heresy that was gaining converts in southern France at the beginning of the thirteenth century.[5] The order grew rapidly.

With an emphasis on winning converts and combating heresy, the Dominicans became the chief defenders of Christian piety and orthodoxy. They took a leading role in medieval university education, dominating the theological faculties of all the leading universities and producing the most important scholastic scholars, including Albertus Magnus (1193–1280) and the foremost philosopher-theologian of the Middle Ages, Thomas Aquinas (1225–74). The Dominicans' emphasis upon combating heresy led to their becoming the chief agents for carrying out the mission of the notorious Inquisition. As the watchdogs of the Roman Catholic faith, they took pride in their nickname "hounds of God," which bore ominous connotations for those like Martin Luther who dared to challenge the authority of the Roman Catholic church hierarchy in matters of religious faith.

5 The Albigensians, also known as *Cathari* ("the Pure"), believed in the existence of two gods: a good god of the spirit and an evil god who ruled the material world.

Within two weeks of its posting on October 31, 1517, the *Ninety-Five Theses* were translated into German and were being printed and distributed throughout the German-speaking areas of the Holy Roman Empire. Within one month the *Theses* were appearing in print throughout Europe. Profit-hungry printers snatched up not only the *Ninety-Five Theses*, but everything written by Martin Luther, his supporters, and his opponents. It is estimated that during the first years after the appearance of the *Ninety-Five Theses* (1517–23), the output of printed works in Germany increased sevenfold, with more than one-half being works written by Martin Luther. The appearance of the printing press in the mid-1450s associated with Johann Gutenberg (c. 1390–1468) was a primary reason why the Reformation occurred at the beginning of the sixteenth century with Martin Luther's challenge, and not at the beginning of the fifteenth century with Jan Hus (1377–1415), who raised many of the same questions voiced by Luther. The growing awareness of Luther's protest was no doubt a major reason why sales of indulgences in Germany began falling off. Church authorities in Rome took notice, and, on August 7, 1518, Luther was ordered to appear in Rome within sixty days to answer to charges of heresy.

The manner in which the late medieval Roman Catholic church dealt with troublesome reformers was to either silence or destroy them. This was possible because medieval society was based upon the acceptance of "one true religion" by all of the people.[6] That one true religion was embodied in the Roman Catholic church, which in turn legitimatized all other institutions, including the state. The Holy Roman Emperor was elected by seven princes, three of whom were archbishops, but he was crowned by either the pope or a representative of the pope. It was this act that legitimatized the emperor's election.

6 Greek Orthodox Christians were regarded as heretics; Muslims were infidels; and Jews were considered to be God's Old Testament Chosen People who one day were expected to give up their resistance and accept Jesus Christ as the long-awaited Messiah.

Since the crowning of Charlemagne (c. 742–814) on Christmas Day in the year 800 by Pope Leo III (d. 816), popes and secular rulers (emperors, kings, princes) debated, even fought wars over, the question of whether final authority within the secular state lay with the pope as Christ's vicar on earth, or whether the pope's authority was limited to religious matters. Had God ordained and given one sword of authority to the pope, or two swords of authority, one to the pope to rule over the church and one to the secular prince to rule over the state? Which institution, papal or princely, happened to dominate at any given moment reflected the relative power of the popes and secular princes at that time.

The zenith of papal power was reached during the pontificate of Innocent III (1160/61–1216). Innocent III claimed that the pope was truly the vicar of Christ on earth with the authority to rule not only the church but the whole world. All secular authority was derived from the pope, who was below God but above man. No individual came as close to achieving such exalted authority as did Innocent III. In 1200, Innocent III placed France under an interdict (i.e., forbade priests to minister the sacraments within a given territory) to force Philip Augustus (1165–1223) to take back his lawful wife, whom he had attempted to divorce. In 1208, the pope placed England under an interdict and excommunicated King John (1167–1216) in 1209, over John's refusal to accept Innocent's choice for archbishop of Canterbury. John was forced to surrender his kingdom to the pope and then receive it back as a fief, becoming a vassal of Innocent III. In 1212, Innocent III imposed his will on the German princes, when he determined the election of Frederick II (1194–1250) as Holy Roman Emperor. In 1208, Innocent III launched a crusade in southern France to wipe out the Albigensian heresy.

The ongoing struggle between the popes and the Holy Roman Emperors was particularly intense. Since the emperors were elected, they tried to build a power base within the Empire on their control of appointments to church offices, and with it, control of the church's wealth within the Holy

Roman Empire. Also, since the Empire included, at least in theory, control of Italy as far south as Rome, it was a perennial goal of the papacy to exert whatever influence it could to assure the election of a weak emperor, and thereby protect the independence of the church. This goal usually harmonized with that of the princes within the Empire. For them the election of a weak emperor assured them maximum control over their territories.

The normal manner in which the late medieval Roman Catholic church dealt with troublesome individuals who challenged church authority was to at first demand their submission. If that failed, then harsher methods were employed. The rebellious individual would be charged with suspicion of heresy and ordered to appear before the appropriate authorities (e.g., the Inquisition) to answer the charges. This allowed the individual an opportunity to confess to error, submit to church authority, and be restored to fellowship. The trial of the Italian scientist, Galileo Galilei (1564–1642) in 1633 is one of the best-known examples of how this procedure might have a "happy" ending. Summoned before the Inquisition in Rome on suspicion of heresy for teaching the Copernican theory of a sun-centered universe, Galileo was interrogated three times before he recanted and signed a confession. Public submission spared him torture and death. Those like Jan Hus and Girolamo Savonarola (1452–98) who refused to submit suffered martyrdom.

For political reasons, Pope Leo X (1475–1521) was not able to move immediately to silence Luther's preaching against indulgences. Effective action required cooperation of the secular authorities, both the Holy Roman Emperor and Luther's own prince, Elector Frederick the Wise (1463–1525), and Leo X could count on neither one. Emperor Maximilan I (1459–1519) was not expected to live much longer, and he hoped to secure the election of his grandson, Charles I (1500–58), king of Spain, as his successor. The election of Charles as Holy Roman Emperor would make him ruler of virtually all of Europe (not to mention the vast Spanish empire in the New World) except France, England,

Portugal, and Scandinavia. The papacy would be surrounded by Habsburg power, and its independence threatened. Since any European prince was eligible, Leo X hoped to block Charles's election and secure the election of Henry VIII (1491–1547), king of England, or perhaps Frederick the Wise. Because Frederick the Wise was one of the seven electors who would elect Maximilian I's successor, Leo X did not wish to offend Frederick who was intent upon seeing his popular professor of theology given a fair hearing inside Germany.

Since Frederick the Wise would not allow Luther to go to Rome and almost certain martyrdom, arrangements were made for Luther to be given a hearing before the papal legate (emissary), Cardinal Thomas Cajetan (1464–1534) in Augsburg. The meeting that took place between October 12 and 14, 1518, was unsuccessful. Cajetan demanded that Luther recant his views and cease causing disruption in the church. Luther refused to recant and returned to Wittenberg, charging that the cardinal was no better qualified to judge his case than a jackass to play a harp.

Since Cardinal Cajetan failed to persuade Luther to recant, the papacy next dispensed Carl von Miltitz (1490–1529), a relative of Frederick the Wise, armed with an assortment of bribes for the elector, should he agree to send Luther to Rome, or at least keep him quiet until after the imperial election. Among the bribes was an additional indulgence of 100 years off purgatory for every saint's relic in Frederick's collection, one of the largest in Europe, housed in the Castle Church at Wittenberg. Also, Frederick was to be rewarded with the coveted Golden Rose, a replica of a rose-and-thorn branch, made of gold and ornamented with gems, and "anointed with holy oil and sprinkled with fragrant incense with the papal benediction." In the accompanying letter from Leo X, the pope urged Frederick to "permit the divine fragrance to enter the innermost heart of Your Excellency, that you may fulfill whatever the aforementioned Carl von Miltitz shall show you."[7] It was even suggested to

---

7 Quoted in Roland Bainton, *Here I Stand: A Life of Martin Luther* (New York: Abingdon Press, 1950), 104.

Frederick that if he cooperated in silencing Luther, he would be permitted to name a cardinal, perhaps even Luther, himself. But Frederick could not be bribed. As one cardinal is reported to have told Miltitz, "You are a pack of fools if you think you can buy the monk from the prince."[8]

Frederick insisted upon Luther being given a fair hearing in Germany. In the end, arrangements were made for Luther to appear before the upcoming meeting of the Imperial Diet (assembly) in Worms on the Rhine.[9] Meanwhile, Luther received an opportunity to debate his theses at the University of Leipzig in June 1519.

The famed Leipzig debate between Martin Luther and Johann Eck (1486–1543), the very able defender of the church from Ingolstadt, was one of the key events in Luther's life. In the course of the debate, Luther appealed to Scripture as his final authority, thus denying the authority of the pope, church councils, or other human institutions, where they conflicted with Scripture as he interpreted it. During the debate, Eck cleverly maneuvered Luther into admitting that some of his opinions agreed with those of Jan Hus, whom a century earlier had been condemned as a heretic by the Council of Constance and turned over to the secular authorities for execution. Luther, in effect, admitted that his views were heretical, as defined by the church.

The Leipzig debate made clear that the real issue Luther was grappling with was the question of whether authority on matters of religious faith and practice belonged to the pope and church tradition or to Scripture alone. During the year 1520, Luther issued an enormous number of publications, but three treatises—*To the Christian Nobility of the German Nation, The Babylonian Captivity of the Church,* and *The Freedom of a Christian*—clarified his developing theology.[10] In

8 Ibid.

9 The Holy Roman Empire did not have a capital. The emperor traveled, holding court in various cities. Hence, each meeting of the Imperial Diet is known by the city and year of that meeting, e.g., Diet of Worms, 1521.

10 See the discussion of these treatises in Chapter 4.

the first he argued that Scripture was the final authority in all areas of faith and practice. In the second he undermined the sacramental system by which the church controlled the laity. He did this by reducing the seven sacraments to only two, baptism and communion, neither of which imparts saving grace. In the last, Luther presented his doctrine of justification by faith alone.

On June 15, 1520, Leo X issued a papal bull, *Exsurge Domine,* formally condemning Luther as a heretic. The issuance of the bull was followed by the burning of Luther's works in Rome. The bull reached Luther in Wittenberg in October. In November, Luther's works were publicly burned in Cologne and other German cities. On December 10, student followers of Luther at the University of Wittenberg ceremoniously burned copies of the canon law of the church, various papal decrees, and publications by Luther's enemies. In a dramatic gesture, Luther cast the papal bull of excommunication into the fire as well. On January 3, 1521, Leo X issued a second bull, *Decet Romanum Pontificem,* confirming Luther's excommunication. Excommunication is a denial of the right to the sacraments, seen as necessary for salvation.

Leo X might excommunicate Luther, but enforcement of the papal bull required the cooperation of the secular state. But here the interests of pope, emperor, and prince were in conflict. Emperor Maximilian I died on January 12, 1519. In the ensuing six months before the imperial election in June, political intrigue became the order of the day. Vast sums of money exchanged hands as the three leading factions tried to influence the electors' choice. It is not known how much Francis I (1494–1547), king of France, expended in his efforts to obtain the imperial crown. The House of Habsburg lavishly spent approximately 1 million gulden, borrowed from the Fugger bank in Augsburg. Leo X was able to sweeten his cash bribes with the offer of church offices. Despite the efforts of Francis I and Leo X, on June 28, the nineteen-year-old Charles I, duke of Burgundy, king of Spain and Naples-Sicily, and with his brother, Archduke Ferdinand

(1503–64), heir to the Habsburg lands of Austria, was elected Charles V, Holy Roman Emperor.

Charles V was a devout Roman Catholic Christian who believed that the defense of Christendom required a strong, universal empire. He was firmly committed to defending Christendom from heretics within and from the infidel Turks (Muslims) without. Charles V's roles as a secular ruler and a faithful son of the church could not always be harmonized. Leo X, likewise, was both spiritual leader of Christendom and the ruler of the Papal States. He was acutely aware of the need to defend the independence of the Papal States, and with it the papacy, against the overwhelming power of the Habsburgs. Both Charles V and Leo X had to deal with conflicting religious and political interests and motives. Increasingly during the sixteenth and seventeenth centuries as the modern nation-states were replacing the medieval feudal monarchies, the interests of the state were given precedence over religious interests by both the secular rulers and the popes.

In addition to the conflicting religious and imperial political interests of both pope and emperor that helped Martin Luther to escape the normal fate of a religious rebel was an additional threat from outside Christendom. In 1520, when Charles was elected Holy Roman Emperor, Suleiman the Magnificient (1494/95–1566) became sultan of the Ottoman Empire. Like Charles V, Suleiman was a scholar, good administrator, and gifted military commander. When war broke out between Francis I and Charles V in 1521, Suleiman seized the opportunity to attack Belgrade, capital of the remaining remnant of the Orthodox Christian Kingdom of Serbia. Southeastern Europe was faced with the nightmare of a possible Muslim invasion.

The war with France and the need to obtain aid from the German princes to meet the Turkish threat weighed heavily upon Charles V's mind as he prepared for the meeting of the Imperial Diet to be held in Worms on the Rhine in April 1521. The Diet of Worms was to provide the stage for the most dramatic and significant event in Luther's career. No doubt for obvious political reasons, Charles V yielded to the persuasion of his uncle, Frederick the Wise, and granted Luther a hearing before the assembled princes of the Holy Roman Empire. Charles V also granted Luther a safe conduct for the journey to Worms and the return journey to Wittenberg. Luther went believing that he would be given an opportunity to defend his views, whereas Charles V intended that Luther would only be given the opportunity to publically recant.

No one knows for certain what Luther said when he appeared before the Diet on April 18, but several accounts of that dramatic event are given. Scholars today doubt if Luther actually spoke those famous words that appear in the earliest printed account, "Here I stand. I can do no other." But they accurately represent his intention. Presented with copies of his publications and asked to give a simple answer to the question of whether or not he wished to recant, Luther replied:

> Since then Your Majesty and your lordships desire a simple reply, I will answer without horns and without teeth. Unless I am convicted by Scripture and plain reason—I do not accept the authority of popes and councils, for they have contradicted each other—my conscience is captive to the Word of God. I cannot and I will not recant anything, for to go against conscience is neither right nor safe. God help me. Amen.[11]

Commotion followed Luther's dramatic speech. He walked from the hall with his hand upraised in gesture of triumph. That a low-ranking priest boldly stood up before the highest ecclesiastical and lay authorities of the day and refused to deny what his conscience said was true, because it came from Scripture supported by reason, was an extraordinary thing.

11 Quoted in Roland Bainton, *Here I Stand: A Life of Martin Luther* (New York: Abingdon Press, 1950), 185.

Although Luther felt he had secured a moral victory at the Diet of Worms, his detractors had also scored a victory. On May 26, the Imperial Diet acting under the authority of the emperor, declared Luther to be an outlaw, and placed him under the ban of the empire. His works were banned, and he was to be hunted down, arrested, and put to death. All who would give him aid and comfort, or who would publish, distribute, or publically approve, defend, or assert Luther's ideas were to be dealt with in the same way.

Frederick the Wise made arrangements to have Luther spirited away to his fortress castle at Wartburg. Luther was allegedly kidnapped by unknown bandits. In fact, this was a ruse arranged by Frederick so as to avoid the charge of harboring a heretic. Luther remained in hiding at Wartburg for eleven months under an assumed identity—"Junker George." He spent much of his time working on his German translation of the New Testament.

In his translation of the New Testament, Luther made use of a Greek translation made by the noted humanist scholar, Desiderius Erasmus of Rotterdam (c. 1466–1536). Erasmus published his Greek New Testament in 1516, together with a revision of the Latin Vulgate text and various philological, theological, and historical notes. In addition to Erasmus's work, Luther also made use of published grammars and glossaries by Johannes Reuchlin (1455–1522), a noted German humanist. After completing a draft of his German translation within eleven weeks, Luther submitted it to his colleague at the University of Wittenberg, Philip Melanchthon (1497–1560). It was first published in September 1522 and became known as the "September Testament."

Luther spent another twelve years translating the Old Testament. He made use of the Latin Vulgate as his basic source text, but also consulted a Hebrew translation of the Psalms and a Hebrew Old Testament. Being aware of his limited knowledge of Greek and Hebrew, Luther sought help from various sources, most notably Philip Melanchthon. Despite numerous interruptions, translation of the Old Testament and Apocrypha was completed in 1532. The first Wittenberg Bible appeared in print in September 1534.

Luther returned to Wittenberg in March 1522. Under an imperial ban, and with a price on his head, Luther remained in Wittenberg preaching and teaching, except for a few brief journeys within the safe environs of central Germany. The Imperial Diet meeting in Nuremberg in 1522 and again in 1524 called for enforcement of the Edict of Worms denouncing Luther. As more and more German princes and cities opted to embrace the new Lutheran teaching, which after 1529 became known as "Protestant," Luther was beyond the reach of the emperor's agents so long as he remained within those territories whose princes supported the expanding Reformation. Those princes who chose to separate from the Roman Catholic church were motivated in part by the desire to strengthen their own authority within their territories vis-à-vis the emperor's claim to sovereignty over the princes and their territories. The times became increasingly difficult for those who followed Luther's teachings. The first Protestant martyrs of the Reformation were burned in Brussels on July 1, 1523.

The years 1524 and 1525 were two of the most momentous in Luther's life. In 1524, Erasmus, as the leading Christian humanist of the day and a former supporter of Luther, yielded to pressure from both lay and ecclesiastical princes, and attacked Luther's teachings in his book, *On Free Will*. Luther responded with *The Bondage of the Will* in the autumn of 1525.[12] The central difference between the Christian humanists and the leaders of the Protestant Reformation was the issue of whether or not education could, apart from divine intervention, produce a virtuous person. Both Christian humanists and Protestant Reformers believed that the church of their day was corrupt and in need of reform. But whereas the former believed that the problem was due to corrupt, or poorly educated individuals in positions of au-

12 *The Bondage of the Will* and the controversy between Luther and Erasmus over free will is discussed in Chapter 5.

thority, the latter believed that the problem was corrupt, or false, doctrine that was the cause of corrupt practice. For the Christian humanists the solution was a better educated clergy. For the Reformers the solution was to remove the bad doctrine that had crept into the church over the centuries by returning to the authority of Scripture. Scripture alone, not Scripture and church tradition, must be the judge of what is, or is not, correct doctrine. The controversy between Luther and Erasmus marked the point at which Christian humanism parted with the Protestant Reformation. Both criticized the corruption in the sixteenth-century church, but differed fundamentally on the cause of the corruption and its cure.13

In January 1525 Luther felt compelled to speak out against his former friend and colleague from the University of Wittenberg, Andreas Bondenstein von Carlstadt (c. 1477–1541). Carlstadt felt that Luther stopped short of following the full teaching of Scripture, that Luther in effect had sold out to the princes. Carlstadt wanted a more radical reformation of worship within the church and relationship between church and state. Luther felt that Carlstadt, along with Thomas Müntzer (d. 1525) and other members of what has been called the Radical Reformation (e.g., the Anabaptists) threatened to disrupt the Reformation. They seemed to de-emphasize the authority of Scripture by emphasizing direct spiritual revelation. Luther responded to this mysticism with a tract titled, *Against the Heavenly Prophets in the Matter of Images and Sacraments.*

Luther was conservative and moderate in his reforms, believing that the laity had to be educated before there were to be sweeping changes in religious practice. While Luther was away at the Wartburg, what would later become the radical or left-wing Reformation began to emerge among some of Luther's followers. In Wittenberg, Carlstadt was the instigator. He began to introduce radical changes in how the Eucharist (Holy Communion) was celebrated, until he abolished its celebration entirely. He refused to baptize infants

13 This is discussed in more detail in Chapter 5.

and renounced his priesthood. His opposition to the use of images in the churches resulted in a popular outburst of iconoclasm, the destruction of images (statues, paintings, etc.) in the churches.

Carlstadt's emphasis on spiritual piety and denigration of material objects, such as images, as aids to worship was carried to even more radical expression by three individuals who came to Wittenberg in December 1521 from the town of Zwickau on the borders of Bohemia. Called the "Zwickau Prophets," they claimed to be receiving revelations directly from God, that superceded the Bible itself. This "extrabiblical revelation" was justified by a belief that the end of the age was near, and God would soon intervene in history to punish the wicked and establish his Kingdom on earth. The growing religious anarchy and threat of social revolution alarmed Frederick the Wise, as well as Luther. Luther feared that a claim to new, direct spiritual revelation would undermine the authority of the Bible as the one certain basis for religious faith and practice. Also, he feared that the growing anarchy and threat of social revolution might cause the princes to intervene and restore order in both the church and society. Such action could mean the end of the reforms Luther so desired.

Against the Heavenly Prophets bitterly attacked his former friend and colleague. Luther refuted Carlstadt's view of the Eucharist as symbolic and defended infant baptism. In doing so, he was not defending the meaning of the two sacraments as taught in the Roman Catholic church, but his understanding of their meaning as taught in Scripture. Luther also accused Carlstadt of encouraging the masses to rebellion by urging the destruction of all images in the church. He defended the authority of the princes, even their authority over the churches within their territories, against any notions of democratic or congregational rule within the churches. For Luther, the Reformation meant reform of the church and religion, not a reformation of the social, economic, or political order of society. As a man of his age, Luther believed that the inequality of people was necessary for the existence of the worldly kingdom.

Luther's abhorrence of rebellion against what he believed to be lawful authority instituted by God was tested by the Peasants' Revolt of 1525. The Peasants' Revolt was but one of many sporadic peasant revolts, not at all uncommon in the late Middle Ages. What distinguished the revolt of 1525 was its scope, its violence, and the brutality with which the lords suppressed it. Another new ingredient was the peasants' appeal to Luther's teachings, especially the doctrine of a priesthood of believers, to justify their revolt. If every individual is his or her own priest, and thereby has direct access to God, then it follows that all people are equal in God's sight. It is easy to see how the peasants could derive from such teaching the conclusion that all people should enjoy social, perhaps even economic, equality on earth. A society based upon the biblical principle of Christian brotherhood, that is, a society that strove for social and economic justice, was antithetical to the hierarchical order of the sixteenth century. Shocked by the threat of anarchy and fearing for the future of the Reformation, Luther responded with *Against the Robbing and Murdering Hordes of Peasants,* a violent attack upon the peasants.[14]

Luther encouraged the princes to suppress the rebellion, not that they needed any encouragement from Luther to do so. The peasants were decisively defeated on May 15, 1525, at the Battle of Frankenhausen near Luther's birthplace. Fifty thousand peasants were massacred by the princes. Before the rebellion was fully quelled, most of the year's crops, hundreds of villages, and about 1,000 castles and monasteries were destroyed. In all, an estimated 100,000 men, women, and children perished. Luther was severely criticized even by his friends and supporters for his harsh words in *Against the Robbing and Murdering Hordes of Peasants,* but he never gave any hint that he regretted the position he took at the height of the rebellion. The peasants felt betrayed by Luther, many turning their backs on the Reformation. The Lutheran movement

14 *Against the Robbing and Murdering Hordes of Peasants* and Luther's reaction to the Peasants's Revolt is discussed in Chapter 6.

was thereafter increasingly controlled by the princes. In subsequent centuries, the Lutheran church would evolve as the state church in those German states that were Protestant.

Not all the events of 1525 were unhappy for Luther. In June he married Katherine von Bora, a former Cistercian nun, who had become one of his followers. They had six children and adopted eleven more. By all accounts, their home was a happy one, and Katie Luther was a great source of strength for her husband.

Church Leader

Martin Luther played an active role in the leadership of the Protestant Reformation. In the fall of 1529, he met with Huyldrich Zwingli (1484–1531), leader of the Reformation in Switzerland. The meeting was called by Philip of Hesse (1504–67) and held at his Marburg Castle. The so-called Marburg Colloquy attempted to bring unity to the various strands of the Protestant Reformation. It ended in failure because neither reformer was willing to compromise on the question of Christ's presence in Communion. Luther firmly believed in Christ's real physical presence in the bread and wine, while Zwingli believed that while Christ was spiritually present at the celebration, Communion was simply a memorial service of his Last Supper.

Luther also had to deal with the growing Radical Reformation, often referred to as Anabaptism. The Anabaptists were condemned by both Roman Catholics and other Protestant groups as well, who often persecuted them with great cruelty. In June 1528, Luther advised the Protestant princes to banish the Anabaptists from their territories, rather than execute them. Later, in 1536, Luther reconsidered, and allowed for the possibility of executing Anabaptists who disturbed the public order or who refused banishment.[15]

15 Luther was not alone in his condemnation of the Anabaptists. In a letter to Henry VIII of England, the Geneva reformer, John Calvin, urged Henry to burn Anabaptists.

In the spring of 1530, the Emperor Charles V summoned the German Lutheran princes to appear before the Imperial Diet meeting in Augsburg to explain their views. Philip Melanchthon drew up a confession of faith with Luther's approval, which was presented to the Diet by the Lutheran princes. Melanchthon's confession was deliberately moderate, too moderate for some of the princes, who hoped it would provide a basis for reconciliation between them and the emperor. By separating from the Roman Catholic church and embracing the new Lutheran faith, and by supporting Luther and defying the imperial ban on Luther and his teachings issued by the Diet of Worms in 1521, the Lutheran princes placed themselves in opposition to both their elected sovereign, the emperor, and the pope. Compromise proved impossible, however, and the emperor gave the Lutheran princes until April 1531, to submit to imperial and Roman Catholic authority. In early 1531, the Protestant princes formed the Schmalkaldic League as a military alliance to meet the threat from Charles V and the Roman Catholic princes within the Holy Roman Empire. The confession drawn up by Melanchthon became the Augsburg Confession, the authoritative doctrinal statement of the Lutheran churches.

Luther introduced a number of reforms in the form of worship in the Protestant churches. They were for the most part not innovations, but revivals of practices lost by the medieval church. They included an emphasis on preaching and teaching of the Bible rather than on the sacrament of Communion. Also, Luther, himself a fine musician, reintroduced music and congregational singing into the service. He published a hymn book in 1524 and even wrote the music and lyrics for one of the best-known hymns, "A Mighty Fortress is Our God."

Luther's health had never been really good. The experience of living continuously under an imperial ban and with a death sentence hanging over his head, together with the trials and tribulations of the Reformation struggle, took their toll on Luther, both physically and emotionally. He was often plagued by digestive and intestinal problems. Beginning in 1527, he suffered from heart problems, uric acid stones, arthritis, and periodic bouts with moderate to severe depression.

Luther's deteriorating health began to affect his work after 1538. Not only did the quantity of his writing drop off, but the tone of his publications changed. They became increasingly blunt, offensive, and even vulgar. Following the death of his beloved daughter Magdalena on September 20, 1542, Luther suffered severe depression. At about the same time, Wittenberg was struck with an outbreak of the plague. These events, together with what he felt was the faithlessness of his beloved Germans, led him to believe that the Last Days prophesied in the Bible were at hand. In this troubled mood Luther wrote the most regrettable pamphlet of his career, *On the Jews and Their Lies.*[16]

Once before in 1523, Luther wrote about the Jews in *That Jesus Was Born a Jew,* a very conciliatory tract that reflected the popular belief that the Jews would be converted to Christianity before the return of Jesus Christ. Luther believed that reform of the church would open the way for the conversion of the Jews. But it did not happen, and Luther grew ever more disappointed and impatient. In 1543, depressed and in poor health, Luther published *On the Jews and Their Lies.* In what Reformation historian Roland Bainton called a "vulgar blast," Luther urged the princes to pack off the Jews to Palestine. If that were not possible, he advised that their synagogues should be burned, all of their books (including Bibles) confiscated, and they should be compelled to make their living from agriculture. Periodic pogroms and persecution of the Jews were common in Christian Europe during the Middle Ages, especially beginning with the Crusades at the end of the eleventh century. In 1492 Jews were ordered to leave Spain, or convert to Christianity. Needless to say, this unfortunate publication of an anti-Jewish pamphlet by the leader of the Reformation has been used by modern anti-Semites to justify their ideology.

16 See the discussion of Luther and the Jews in Chapter 6.

Luther was not well, when in February, 1546, he left Wittenberg for Mansfeld to arbitrate a dispute between two brothers, the counts of Mansfeld. On his return journey, he stopped off in Eisleben, where he was born. There, he preached his final sermon, to which he appended an "Admonition Against the Jews," whom he now blamed for his illness. The events surrounding his death in the early hours of February 18, 1546, are disputed. Whether he died in his sleep or after uttering some last words is not known for certain. His body was taken to Wittenberg, where it was buried on February 22, in the church on whose door he had posted his *Ninety-Five Theses* on October 31, 1517.

Summary

Throughout church history leaders have risen from among the least likely candidates to guide the church through difficult times. Martin Luther was one such individual. Of very humble background, Luther's parents sacrificed to give him a good education. They meant for him to have a career in the legal profession, but Luther felt called to service in the church. His need to understand how God saves the sinner, and how the redeemed sinner can have assurance of salvation, put Luther on a collision course with the church hierarchy. In 1517, he posted his Ninety-Five Theses, *a challenge to the church's teaching on salvation. Condemned as a heretic by the papacy in 1521, Luther became the leader of the Protestant Reformation. Restricted to Wittenberg and those safe areas of Germany where the death sentence decreed by the Diet of Worms in 1521 could not be enforced, Luther devoted his remaining years, until his death in 1546, translating the Bible, writing commentaries on the books of the Bible, and turning out an endless list of publications on theology and Christians in society. He published devotional works that touch the reader's heart, as well as controversial works that leave the reader, especially today's reader, disturbed, if not angry. Martin Luther may not have been a man for all seasons, but he was the man of the hour to launch the reformation of the church in the sixteenth century.*

Key Events

1483   Martin Luther is born to Hans and Margaretta Luther on November 10 in Eisleben, Saxony (Germany). He is baptized in the Roman Catholic church of Sts. Peter and Paul on the following day.

1505   Luther enters the monastery of the Augustinian Hermits in Erfurt.

1517   Luther posts his *Ninety-Five Theses,* an invitation to debate indulgences, on the door of the Castle Church in Wittenberg on October 31, the eve of All Saints Day.

1520   Pope Leo X issues a papal bull, *Exsurge Domine,* excommunicating Luther.

1521   Luther appears before the Imperial Diet of the Holy Roman Empire in Worms, where on April 17, he makes his famous "Here I Stand" speech.

1525   Luther marries Katherina von Bora on June 13.

1534   The first edition of Luther's complete German translation of the Bible is published.

1546   Luther dies on February 18 in Eisleben. He is buried in the Castle Church in Wittenberg on February 22.

CHAPTER TWO

Salvation
in the Late Middle Ages

At the heart of the Protestant Reformation was the question of salvation, or how a sinner comes to be justified before God. It was for the Reformers, especially Martin Luther, to rediscover the gospel proclaimed by the New Testament church, that is, that salvation is by grace through faith in Jesus Christ. The early church proclaimed that salvation was a free and wholly unmerited gift of God's grace, whereby God attributes the righteousness of Christ to the individual who is inherently sinful on the basis of his faith in Christ, thus justifying that person in God's sight. This biblical tenet had become obscured by the medieval church's fusion of justification with sanctification. Originating as an event, an instant, when God proclaims the believer righteous on the basis of his faith in Christ, justification came to mean a process by which people attempt to earn their salvation by doing enough good works to offset their sins. Thus instead of salvation being a free gift of God's grace, it came to be laden with the oppressive burden of "works-righteousness."

Salvation in the Early Church

The way of salvation as proclaimed by the early church is first presented in the gospels, and then spelled out by the Apostle Paul, especially in his letters to the Romans and the Galatians. There salvation is presented as an event, a one-time act of God's grace, whereby the sinner, having put his faith in the redemption of Jesus Christ's death on the cross, becomes righteous (i.e., justified) by God. This was the basic principle rediscovered by Luther in his study of the letters of the Apostle Paul: salvation from sin is freely offered to everyone who believes.

Paul says that when God pronounces a sinner justified, or made righteous, the sinner passes from death to eternal life. Hence God's grace has already secured the believer's eternal destiny. Because of Christ's atonement for the sins of humankind, the believer may stand before God without fear of guilt or penalty. Thus in answer to the Philippian jailer's question, "Sirs, What must I do to be saved?," Paul and Silas responded: "Believe in the Lord Jesus, and you will be saved . . . " (Acts 16: 30,31a [NIV][1]). In one sense, salvation has already been achieved by believers. There is also a sense in which salvation is an ongoing process in the present life of believers—referred to as sanctification.

In his letter to the Romans, Paul explains that sanctification is the lifelong process in which believers are empowered by the Holy Spirit to resist temptation and daily become more like Christ. Though believers will stumble and sin, they need not feel that their salvation is thereby lost or attempt to make atonement by self-punishment. Rather, the believers need only to confess their sins, and God will forgive them. Thus, the ongoing process of sanctification is distinct from the one-time act of justification.

But the early church also taught that there is a sense in which salvation is a future event. Believers look forward to a future glory, when the effects of the fall of Adam and Eve (and thus of all humankind) will be overcome, and believers, made righteous through Jesus Christ, will be glorified with Him. Liberated from sin's presence, believers will be restored to the image and likeness of God in which they were created and will enjoy eternal life with him. Thus salvation as presented in the Bible and taught by the early church had a past, present, and future meaning.

Salvation in the Medieval Church

Luther and the other Protestant Reformers believed that the distinction between justification and sanctification was

1 New International Version (NIV)

blurred and eventually lost during the Middle Ages, roughly the fifth through fifteenth centuries. Augustine, bishop of Hippo (354–430), one of the early Latin Church Fathers in the West, obscured the distinction between the one-time act of justification and the ongoing process of sanctification in the life of the believer. Ignorant of Greek, he interpreted the Greek *dikaioun* (Latin, *justificari*) as meaning "to make righteous." He rejected the possibility of its meaning, "to pronounce righteous," as later translated by Martin Luther.[2] Of course Luther had the benefit of Erasmus's Greek New Testament, first published in 1516.

For Augustine, the soul of the individual was permeated with righteousness at baptism. Augustine defended the practice of baptizing infants, which was already common by the end of the second century, and by the end of the fifth century had displaced adult believer's baptism as the normal practice of the church. Justification became a lifelong process of growing in righteousness in order that after death, God might pronounce the believer justified (i.e., saved).[3] Thus Augustine read in the teaching of the Apostle Paul a combination of justification and sanctification. Augustine's interpretation became the accepted medieval view, reaffirmed in the teaching of Thomas Aquinas, the foremost scholastic theologian of the Middle Ages.

For Aquinas, the believer is justified by God's grace, which is received through the sacraments (Baptism, Eucharist, etc.), and which permeates the soul of the believer. Therefore, justification as understood by the medieval church was the ongoing "production of a state," not the "acquirement of a status," and was dependent upon a faithful observance of the sacraments administered to the believer by the church.[4]

---

2 Peter Toon, "Justification" in J. D. Douglas, ed., *New 20th-Century Encyclopedia of Religious Knowledge,* 2d ed. (Grand Rapids, MI: Baker Book House, 1991), 474.
3 Ibid.
4 Ian Sellers, "Justification" in J. D. Douglas, ed. *The New International Dictionary of the Christian Church,* rev. ed., (Grand Rapids, MI: Zondervan Publishing House, 1978), 557.

This ongoing gift of the Holy Spirit required faith on the part of the recipient. Thus when the medieval Roman Catholic church said that salvation was by faith in Jesus Christ, it did not teach that salvation was by faith alone. This distinction was the all-important point of departure between the Roman Catholic church and the Protestant Reformation. Luther and the Protestant Reformation as a whole held the biblical position of the early church, that salvation was achieved by grace through faith, alone.

Salvation in the Late Medieval Church

To understand the late medieval church's teachings with respect to salvation, we need to look at the scholastic theologian, Gabriel Biel (c. 1420–95). Although Biel died twelve years after Luther's birth and thirty-four years before Luther was to launch the Protestant Reformation, his life and teachings influenced Luther in several ways. Both Luther and Biel were influenced by the Brethren of the Common Life, Luther as a student in one of its schools, and Biel as prior of the brotherhouse at Butzbach (1470) and later at Urach (1479). The Brethren of the Common Life was a popular lay movement in Germany and the Netherlands during the fourteenth and fifteenth centuries that emphasized educating poor youth, while stressing personal piety and communion with God. It is often regarded as one of the movements that contributed to the coming of the Protestant Reformation.

Gabriel Biel was also the last great follower of the scholastic theologian and philosopher, William of Ockham (c. 1280–c. 1349). William of Ockham was the founder of nominalism as a systematic philosophy. In contrast to Thomas Aquinas and the other realist scholastic theologians, the nominalists held that God was above reason and could be known only by faith. The nominalists referred to their philosophy as the *via moderna,* or "modern way," in contrast to the *via antiqua,* or "old way" of the followers of Aquinas. Luther came under the influence of the *via moderna* as a student at the University of Erfurt, and later as a professor at the University of Wittenberg.

The universities of Erfurt and Wittenberg were both strongholds of Ockhamist teaching. After entering the Augustinian monastery at Erfurt, Luther devoted himself to the study of theology under Johannes Nathin (d. 1529), who occupied the Augustinian chair at the university. Nathin had been a younger colleague of Gabriel Biel for several years at the University of Tübingen. As Luther's major professor, as well as brother monk, Johannes Nathin must have had a profound influence on Luther's intellectual development. However, it is difficult to properly assess that influence. Either Nathin did not leave any writings behind or did not in fact publish anything, for nothing exists by this key figure in Luther's life.

There can be no doubt, however, about Biel's influence. Philip Melanchthon, Luther's colleague at the University of Wittenberg and his successor as leader of the Lutheran movement, testified that Luther had studied Biel's *Exposition* on the canon of the Mass and other writings so thoroughly that he could quote whole pages from memory. It is perhaps from Ockham, by way of Biel, that Luther came to his concept of Christ's presence in the bread and wine of the Eucharist (a view known as consubstantiation), whereby the elements remain bread and wine.

Although Luther was no doubt influenced by Gabriel Biel and the nominalists, Luther eventually rejected most of their teaching. As the distinguished church historian Bard Thompson suggests, to fully understand what Luther *opposed*, we must try to understand what Biel *proposed*. Eventually, Biel's teaching with respect to salvation represented the teaching of the Roman Catholic church at the beginning of the sixteenth century, that is, that salvation is the product of a cooperative effort on the part of God and the individual.

Thompson imagines Biel being approached by one of his distraught parishioners, asking him how he might be saved. Biel would almost certainly have advised the individual:

Do your very best, and sometime soon God will bestow
upon you the habit of grace. Continue to do your very best,
and that habit of grace will enable you to do good works
that God will find full of merit, which will finally offset all
your sins and make you "right" with God.[5]

It is clear that underlying Biel's thought is the assumption of
human free will. Biel believed that the Fall diminished the
pleasure that one might receive from doing good works, but
did not destroy one's freedom to make moral choices. Fallen
mankind retained freedom of will.

Biel saw life as a pilgrimage, at the end of which was
eternal life. Without God's help through grace, the pilgrim's
goal of salvation could not be attained. But the pilgrim could
be optimistic, for the pilgrim was able to solicit God's help
by doing his or her very best. In response to this, God would
come to the aid of the pilgrim.

God, on his part, finds himself obliged, by an obligation to
which, so to speak, he had freely committed himself, to as-
cribe to that person the merit of congruence (*meritum de
congruo*). "Congruence" here refers to the point at which
human effort and God's help coincide. God now proceeds
to award that person the *habitus*—the status or habit—of
grace, enabling him or her to perform works that God deems
to be works of genuine merit, meritorious works that will
advance him or her toward the goal of perfection and eternal life.[6]

5 Bard Thompson, *Humanists and Reformers: A History of the Renaissance and Reformation* (Grand Rapids: William B. Eerdmans
Publishing Co., 1996), 386. Here and in what follows, I am following Bard Thompson's summary of the contrast between Biel
and Luther (Ibid., 385–394). The question of free will is what also
separated Luther from the Christian humanists, for example,
Erasmus. See the discussion of Luther's *The Bondage of the Will*
in Chapter 5.
6 Ibid., 386.

Thus, as one goes through life in a "habit of grace," able to perform good works that God deems meritorious, one is able to accumulate enough good works to offset the burden of one's sins. In the end, the pilgrim is "made right," or justified before God.

For Biel, and for the late medieval church, salvation, or justification, is from first to last a process of "making good," which is possible because sinners possess the ability, with God's help, to perform good works deemed meritorious by God. This system entirely depends on the individual's possession of a free will. But from his study of the New Testament, especially the Pauline epistles, Luther concluded that human will was so totally corrupted by the Fall, that he or she simply did not possess the ability to do any righteous act.

Luther's Understanding of Salvation

The central theme of the New Testament is that God offered his own Son, Jesus Christ, as a sacrifice for all the sins of fallen humanity. Luther's view was that rather than trying to earn one's salvation through good works, the individual sinner must put his faith in Jesus Christ and will then participate in Christ's righteousness. Thus according to Luther's understanding of the New Testament, salvation is by faith alone, not faith plus good works.

A question then arose: if faith is necessary for salvation, how do sinners who lack a free will obtain such saving faith? Again, Luther looked to the New Testament, especially Paul's letter to the Romans. There he discovered that faith comes from hearing the news of Jesus Christ and his atoning death on the cross (Rom. 10:17). Luther believed that the gospel may be preached by anyone. It was not a treasure dispensed by priests who stand in a line going back to St. Peter, as claimed in the Petrine Theory, whereby the pope was the successor of St. Peter and possessor of the keys to heaven and hell. Rather, whoever told the news of salvation through faith in Jesus Christ was in the apostolic succession. And wherever that news was preached, there was the church. Since in Luther's view the gospel of salvation by grace through faith in Jesus Christ is the main thrust of the Scriptures, Christianity depended upon the Bible, not the Bible plus the decisions of church councils, the reasoning of theologians, or on papal pronouncements.

But again Luther wondered, if salvation is dependent upon faith that comes from hearing and believing the gospel, how can sinners who do not possess a free will believe? Luther concluded the only answer is that faith itself is a gift from God. Only as the individual is empowered by the Holy Spirit can he or she believe. Hence, for him, salvation is wholly a gift of God's grace. Then the question arises, if salvation is entirely a gift of God's grace, why are some saved and others not? Here Luther agrees with Augustine and the other mainline Reformers like John Calvin (1509–64), that God, in his sovereignty, chooses, or elects, to save some, while he leaves others to suffer the just rewards of their sins.

In the Preface to his commentary on the book of Romans, Luther reveals his belief in the doctrine of *predestination:*

> In chapters 9, 10, and 11, Paul deals with the eternal providence of God. It is by this providence that it was first decided who should, and who should not, have faith; who should conquer sin, and who should not be able to do so. This is a matter which is taken out of our hands, and is solely at God's disposal—so that we might be truly righteous.[7]

For Luther, then, God's grace is not given to sinners through the sacraments. Rather, it is the demonstration of God's favor towards sinners, given freely, and in no way dependent upon anything sinners have done or could possibly do.

7 John Dillenberger, ed., *Martin Luther: Selections From His Writings* (New York: Doubleday & Company, 1961), 32.

Summary

At the heart of the Reformation was the issue of how one is justified before God, that is, how one achieves eternal salvation. To properly understand Martin Luther and the great volume of his works, the twenty-first century reader must understand the contrast between what the late medieval church taught regarding salvation as opposed to the teachings of the early New Testament church. The Roman Catholic church of Luther's day taught that salvation was achieved by faith plus goods works, that is, the individual cooperating with God in his or her salvation. Luther's study of the Scriptures led him to conclude that Adam and Eve's fall from grace had so corrupted human will, that salvation could only be a free gift from God. For Luther, salvation was achieved by grace through faith in Jesus Christ alone.

Key Events

354–430   Augustine, bishop of Hippo and one of the early Church Fathers, reinterprets the teaching of the early church by combining justification and sanctification.

1224–74   Building on Augustine, Thomas Aquinas teaches that the believer is justified by God's grace dispensed through the sacraments, especially the Eucharist.

c. 1420–95 Gabriel Biel's teaching best represents the mechanical sacramentalism of the medieval church on the eve of the Protestant Reformation.

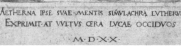

Top left: Martin Luther as a monk by Lucas Cranach the Elder. Louvre, Paris, France. Photo Credit: Erich Lessing / Art Resource, NY; Top right: Frederick the Wise, Elector and Duke of Saxony by Albrecht Dürer. Gemaeldegalerie, Staatliche Museen zu Berlin, Berlin Germany. Photo Credit: Bildarchiv Preussischer Kulturbesitz / Art Resource, NY; Bottom left: Erasmus of Rotterdam, c. 1523 by Hans Holbein the Younger. Louvre, Paris, France. Photo Credit: Erich Lessing / Art Resource, NY; Bottom right: Pope Leo X with Cardinals Giulio de'Medici and Luigi de'Rossi, c. 1517, by Raphael. Uffizi, Florence Italy. Photo Credit: Alinari / Art Resource, NY.

⊕ CHAPTER THREE ⊕
The Ninety-Five Theses

Background

The medieval Christian had very little fear of hell. The keys to heaven and hell had been given to St. Peter, and according to the Petrine Theory,[1] were possessed by St. Peter's successors, the popes. Through the sacrament of penance the penitent sinner could confess his or her sins to a priest, who then pronounced absolution. The confessed sinner was forgiven the guilt and eternal punishment that was due for sins committed. Although the guilt and eternal punishment for confessed sins was forgiven by God, there remained a burden of temporal punishments that had to be satisfied, either in this life through good works or after death in purgatory. Since all but the saints could count on spending an indefinite time in purgatory making atonement before passing on to heavenly bliss, it was purgatory that the individual most feared. The least punishment imposed in purgatory was thought to be worse than the worst punishment imposed by the church in this life. Also, the time spent in purgatory could be indefinite. A medieval pilgrim, for example, who viewed the relics on display in the Castle Church at Wittenberg, was forgiven a total of 1,902,202 years and 270 days in purgatory. Pilgrims wondered how many years of purgatory might yet remain.

1 The Petrine Theory is based on Mathew 16: 13–19. In Verse 19, Jesus says to Peter: "I will give you the keys of the kingdom of heaven; whatever you bind on earth will be bound in heaven, and whatever you loose on earth will be loosed in heaven [NIV]." The Roman Catholic church teaches that Peter was the first bishop of Rome and passed the authority believed to have been given to him by Jesus in this passage on to his successors, i.e., the popes.

The souls in purgatory were not left without assistance from the medieval church. Prayers and masses could be said on behalf of those in purgatory. Often wealthy individuals would endow masses to be said on behalf of departed family members. Also, the authority of the pope to bind and loose people from sins extended into purgatory. This authority was exercised through the issuance of indulgences. An indulgence was the remission of all or part of the temporal (meaning limited, not eternal) punishment owed for sins after guilt already had been forgiven. In 1476, Pope Sixtus IV (1471–84) extended indulgences to include those souls in purgatory.

As fear of purgatory fed the demand for indulgences, the medieval popes found them a convenient means of enhancing their wealth and power. The period of the Crusades against the Muslims in the Middle East from 1095 to the end of the thirteenth century saw a tremendous growth in the demand for indulgences. Pope Urban II (1088–99) granted a plenary indulgence, providing complete relief from purgatory for all who would join the Crusades to liberate the Holy Land. By the end of the twelfth century, plenary indulgences were being offered to those who contributed financially to a Crusade, for example, by paying the costs of a crusader. Under Pope Innocent III (1198–1216) the extent of the indulgence was related to the amount of the contribution.

With the waning of the Crusades, new forms of indulgences were found in order to ensure the steady flow of revenue into the church coffers. No other sources of revenue were so lucrative. In 1294, the papacy began issuing confessional letters to wealthy individuals. The purchaser/possessor was entitled to a once-in-a-lifetime full remission of temporal punishments from any priest, or a full remission upon his or her death. In 1300, Pope Boniface VIII (1294–1303) established a jubilee indulgence, a full remission of all temporal punishments to all pilgrims who visited the graves of the apostles in Rome during the year of jubilee. By the end of the fifteenth century, indulgences were offered for sale by traveling indulgence vendors. These papal "pardoners" were favorite targets for medieval satirists, as for example in Geoffrey Chaucer's (1340–1400) *Canterbury Tales.* So commercialized had the trade in indulgences become, that even church authorities referred to it, without any sense of embarrassment, as the "holy trade," or *sacrum negotium.*

The trade in indulgences was supported theologically by the doctrine of the Treasury of Merit, first formulated in the thirteenth century. According to this doctrine, there existed in heaven a storehouse, or treasure chest, of excess merit accumulated by Jesus Christ and the saints, whose good works far exceeded what God demanded. As the successor of St. Peter and possessor of the keys, the pope could draw upon this treasury of merit to grant indulgences. It was merely a kind of bookkeeping transaction, whereby some merit was withdrawn from one account and credited to another account. By Luther's day, an individual could be assured that the punishment for his sins, or those of some loved one in purgatory, could be cancelled merely by purchasing an indulgence.

In 1510, Pope Julius II (1503–13) announced a jubilee indulgence. The proceeds from the sale of indulgences was to finance the construction of St. Peter's basilica in Rome. It was the revival of this indulgence by Pope Leo X in 1515, and, in particular, the offensive and even blasphemous sales tactics employed by Johann Tetzel (c.1465–1519), the experienced Dominican seller of indulgences, that aroused Luther's anger.

Tetzel was forbidden by Luther's prince, Elector Frederick the Wise, to sell indulgences inside Electoral Saxony. His reasons were perhaps initially more economic than pious. Frederick's collection of relics and the indulgences attached to them were a great source of revenue for the support of his university. Any indulgences purchased from the traveling indulgence sellers would only result in a loss of revenue. The financial exploitation of Germany by the papacy was a widespread grievance among the Germans in the late Middle Ages.

Denied entrance to Electoral Saxony, Tetzel set up shop in Juterbog and Zerbst, just over the border some thirty-five kilometers from Wittenberg. Members of Luther's parish returned from Juterborg with tales of how forgiveness of sin and its penalties without the need for confession or contrition could be purchased, even for souls in purgatory. An indulgence slip could be purchased, they were told, that would compel a priest to grant the bearer absolution or face excommunication by none other than Tetzel himself. When Luther heard such tales from those for whom he felt a responsibility as their parish priest, he was compelled to speak out, not against the doctrine of indulgences, but their abuse by Tetzel and his associates.

Tetzel was acting on behalf of Albert von Hohenzollern (1490–1545), archbishop of Magdeburg, administrator of Halberstadt and archbishop and elector of Mainz. In order to hold two archbishoprics concurrently, Albert had obtained a dispensation from the pope, since holding two archbishoprics was a clear violation of canon law. To obtain the dispensation and the archbishopric of Mainz, Albert paid the papacy the sum of 10,000 ducats, a sum he borrowed from the Fugger bank in Augsburg. To enable Albert to repay his loan, Leo X authorized Albert to sell indulgences within his territories for a period of eight years. The proceeds from the sales were to be divided equally between Albert and the papacy. Albert would use his share to repay his loan from the Fuggers. Leo would use his share to complete the construction of St. Peter's Basilica.

As already indicated the terms of the indulgence were especially generous in order to assure a maximum of income. Also, Tetzel and the other sellers were given precise instructions as to how much they were to charge for an indulgence: "princes of the blood twenty-five guilders, prelates and barons ten guilders, the better-class citizenry six guilders, the poorer citizenry one guilder, down to the ordinary people who could get a letter of indulgence for half a quarter of a guilder."[2]

2 Richard Friedenthal, *Luther: His Life and Times* (New York: Harcourt Brace Jovanovich, 1967), 130.

The *Ninety-Five Theses*

On October 31, 1517, Martin Luther, accompanied by one of his students, Johann Schneider of Eisleben, made the fifteen-minute walk from the Augustinian Cloister to the Castle Church in Wittenberg. On the eve of All Saints, Wittenberg would bulge with pilgrims waiting for the church doors to open so that they could walk through its halls viewing and venerating the vast collection of holy relics assembled by Elector Frederick the Wise. Luther carried a rolled-up document in one hand, a hammer in the other. When he arrived at the church's north entrance, where the large wooden door served as the university bulletin board, he nailed the document to the door.[3]

The document known ever since as the *Ninety-Five Theses* was written in Latin and bore the title, *Disputation on the Power and Efficacy of Indulgences.* It was an invitation to the academic community to debate the ninety-five theses it contained regarding indulgences. This event marks the beginning of the Protestant Reformation. The theses circulated among Luther's friends at first, but by the end of November or early December 1517, they were appearing in print in both Latin and German throughout Germany and even in Switzerland. Archbishop Albert apparently read them in late November, and then passed them along to the papal court. Pope Leo X did not take them too seriously at first. "Friar Martin has talent," he is supposed to have said, "that is why they're jealous of him. All this fuss is nothing more than the

3 Recent scholarship questions whether the *Ninety-Five Theses* was in fact posted on October 31, 1517, or perhaps later in mid or late November. It is possible that it was never in fact posted on the church door. Luther did, however, send a copy accompanied by a letter to Archbishop Albert and Bishop Jerome Schulze of Brandenburg on October 31. A copy of the letter sent to Albert has survived. See the discussion of the event in, e.g., Martin Brecht, *Martin Luther: His Road to Reformation, 1483–1521* (Minneapolis: Fortress Press, 1985), 200–202.

usual monkish rivalry." Some sources record him comment-
ing, "Never mind, it's only a drunken German, who will feel
differently when he sobers up."4

When Luther drew up his theses, he believed that the
pope and his archbishop were unaware of the shocking mis-
representations of indulgences preached by Tetzel and other
indulgence sellers. From his letter to Archbishop Albert,
Luther clearly believed that if the archbishop were made aware
of the abuses, he would correct them. Luther was not at this
point attacking the church's system of indulgences. He believed that what penances the church imposed, it could also
commute. In a letter explaining the *Ninety-Five Theses* that
Luther sent to his bishop in February 1518, he expressed
the belief that the church had abandoned New Testament
Christianity and had become woefully ignorant in theological terms. If the church would make itself aware of this, then
God would bring it a reformation.

Content of the *Ninety-Five Theses*

Luther made his intention clear in the brief preamble to
the *Ninety-Five Theses*. They were to be discussed at a public
disputation to be held in Wittenberg and chaired by "rever-
end father Martin Luther, Master of Arts and Sacred Theology and regularly appointed Lecturer on these subjects at
that place."5 Those of the academic community who could
not be present for the debate were invited to submit their
opinions in writing. No debate ever took place, however,
since there was initially no response from the academic community or the church hierarchy to the posting of the theses.

The first four theses deal with the true nature of penance. Here Luther asserted that, in contrast to the practice

4 Quoted in Edith Simon, *Luther Alive: Martin Luther and the
Making of the Reformation* (London: Hoddar and Stoughton,
1968), 142.
5 All quotations from the *Ninety-Five Theses* are from the translation by C. M. Jacobs (revised by Harold J. Grimm) and found in
volume 31 of Jaroslav Pelikan and Helmut T. Lehmann, gen. eds.,
Luther's Works (Philadelphia: Muhlenberg Press, 1957), 25–33.

of treating penance as a mercantile transaction (selling indulgences), in the New Testament true repentance is a characteristic of the believer's change in lifestyle, whereby the sinner, having become a believer, turns away from sin to embrace a life in search of righteousness. That is what Luther believed Jesus Christ meant when he says "repent" in Matthew 4:17. The implication was that the sacrament of penance as administered by the clergy interfered with true repentance, since it was motivated by a desire to avoid punishment in purgatory.

Theses five through seven deal with the pope's authority to remit both guilt and penalties for sin. Luther asserted that the pope had authority to remit only those penalties which he had authority to impose, or which result from canon law. Since Roman Catholic theology makes a distinction between the "guilt" and the "penalty" for sin, Luther asserted that only God can remit (i.e., release the sinner from) guilt. The pope may pronounce remission of guilt, but only in God's name. In thesis seven, Luther asserted that God would forgive the sins of only those whom he first humbles and makes submissive to his vicar, the priest.

Luther next turned his attention to the pope's authority over purgatory in theses eight through twenty-nine, striking a blow at indulgences for the dead. Whatever penance could be imposed by the church, Luther held, can be imposed only on the living: therefore whatever penalties have been imposed are cancelled by death. The belief that penalties imposed in this life could be extended into purgatory was a corruption of doctrine which, Luther asserted in thesis eleven, "crept into the church while the bishops were sleeping," an allusion to Matthew 13:25. Luther did not deny the existence of purgatory, only the church's (i.e., the pope's) authority over it. The pope might intercede with God on behalf of the souls in purgatory, but God was under no obligation to respond positively to the pope's prayers. In denying the pope's authority over purgatory, Luther was in agreement with the medieval popes.

Luther posited that since the pope had no authority over the souls in purgatory and could only intercede on their behalf through prayer, the pope's use of the words "plenary remission of all penalties," referred only to those penalties he had imposed. Luther here gave the pope the benefit of the doubt, or perhaps truly believed that Leo X was unaware of the claims being made in his name by Tetzel and his fellow indulgence vendors. In theses twenty-one and twenty-seven, Luther accused the hawkers of indulgences of being in error and preaching "only human doctrines," when they claim that the indulgences they are offering for sale can release the purchaser from penalties suffered in purgatory.

In theses thirty through forty, Luther turned his attention to the question of indulgences for the living. In thesis thirty-six, Luther asserted that "any truly repentant Christian has a right to full remission of penalty and guilt, even without indulgence letters." He goes on in thesis thirty-seven to point out that such forgiveness is freely given by God as a part of "all the blessings of Christ and the church." Luther did not mean that the pope's pronouncement of forgiveness is to be ignored, for it was a proclamation of what God has already done. But, instead, those who trusted in indulgences for certainty of salvation apart from any true repentance were putting their faith in a false and unchristian doctrine. Hence they would suffer eternal damnation along with those who preached such false doctrine (Thesis 32).

In theses forty-one through fifty-one, Luther contrasted good works motivated by true mercy and love with the purchase of indulgences. Luther stated that the Christian grows spiritually by acts of true love and mercy, but he who ignores others in need and expends his resources on purchasing indulgences to the neglect of the needy or his own family, "does not buy papal indulgences but God's wrath" (Theses 43–46).

Regarding the building of St. Peter's Basilica from the sale of indulgences, Luther believed that if the pope only "knew the exactions of the indulgence preachers, he would rather that the basilica of St. Peter were burned to ashes than built up with the skin, flesh, and bones of his sheep" (Thesis 50). Christians were to be taught, said Luther, that the pope "would and should" wish not only to give of his own re-sources, but to sell St. Peter's Basilica if necessary and give the proceeds to those poor souls "from whom certain indul-gence hawkers cajole money" (Thesis 51).

Luther then turned his attention in theses fifty-three through fifty-five to how the preaching of indulgences had displaced the preaching of the true gospel. Here again he assumed that the pope was ignorant of the abuses. Luther contrasted the Treasury of Merit, from which indulgences were supposedly drawn, something which is "not sufficiently discussed or known among the people of Christ" (Thesis 56), with the "true treasure of the church," which is "the most holy gospel of the glory and grace of God" (Thesis 62). Luther held that the gospel was not as loved as the idea of indulgences, because the gospel humbles the proud in order that they might be redeemed, while indulgences mis-lead the proud into thinking that they can purchase redemp-tion (Theses 63 & 64). Whereas formerly the church fished for men of wealth with the nets of the true gospel, Luther accused it of using indulgences as "nets with which one now fishes for the wealth of men" (Theses 65 & 66).

Among the abuses preached on behalf of indulgences that Luther mentioned is the claim that even if one had vio-lated Mary, the mother of Jesus Christ, he could be forgiven by purchasing an indulgence. Such a claim is madness, said Luther, since "papal indulgences cannot remove the very least of venial sins as far as guilt is concerned" (Thesis 76). Further, Luther charges in thesis seventy-nine that it was blasphemy to assert, as some indulgence sellers did, that the crosses they erect adorned with the papal coat of arms are "equal in worth to the cross of Christ." Those "bishops, curates, and theologians" who allow such abuses to be spread among the people will answer to God.

In a series of rhetorical questions in theses eighty-two through eighty-nine, Luther presented the shrewd questions raised by common people against the indulgence traffic. Why did the pope not empty purgatory out of love, rather than releasing some souls for the sake of money with which to build a church? Why did he not cancel the endowed masses for the dead for whom indulgences have been granted and return the funds to their owners? Why did the pope refuse to release a pious soul from purgatory out of love but would do so for a payment from an impious person? Why did the pope not build St. Peter's Basilica out of his own vast wealth rather than with the funds obtained from poor believers? Luther then said that to respond to these objections with repression rather than reason exposes the pope and the church to ridicule while making Christians unhappy. However, again in thesis ninety-one, Luther pulls back from charging Pope Leo X with responsibility for the abuses. If indulgences, he claims, "were preached according to the spiritual intention of the pope, all these doubts would be readily resolved. Indeed, they would not exist."

In the final four theses (92–95), Luther alluded to Jeremiah 6:14 in condemning those who preach a cheap grace and a false security: "Away then with those prophets who say to the people of Christ, 'Peace, peace,' and there is no peace" (Thesis 92). Instead, he calls upon Christians to take up their cross and follow Jesus Christ, "their head, through penalties, death, and hell" (Thesis 94). Only by following the example of Jesus Christ and forsaking the false gospel of peace and security through the purchase of indulgences could Christians find true peace and security. This marked the beginning of Luther's budding "theology of the Cross." At the heart of this new theology, as Luther suggested earlier in theses forty-one through fifty-one, was the desire to do God's will and serve one's brethren through works of true love and mercy.

Significance

The significance of the *Ninety-Five Theses* does not lie in its attack upon indulgences. As late as 1541, Luther insisted that his intent was to call attention to abuses, not to attack either the doctrine of indulgences or the pope. Luther was not the first to question indulgences. During the little more than a century before Luther's *Ninety-Five Theses,* a number of leading figures from within the church denounced indulgences. Among them were John Wycliffe (c. 1320–84), Jan Hus, and Johannes von Wesel (c. 1400–81).

The significance of the *Ninety-Five Theses* lay in the fact that in this document Luther presented for the first time since the period of the New Testament church a new way of viewing Christian life, not as a pilgrimage in pursuit of salvation, but as a desire to follow in the footsteps of Jesus Christ. In contrasting his new theology of the cross with the works-righteousness preached by the medieval church, Luther, in the words of the Christian humanist Erasmus, committed two sins: "He has attacked the crown of the pope and the bellies of the monks."[6] By questioning the pope's authority, Luther forced the church hierarchy to engage him in a struggle that would launch the Protestant Reformation.

Summary

It was not the prospect of hell that terrified the medieval Christian. Hell could easily be avoided by careful observance of the sacramental system of the church. Rather, it was purgatory that the Christian feared most. It was not possible to earn enough merit in this life to avoid spending an indefinite amount of time in purgatory making up the deficit in works left after one's death in atonement for sin. One method of shortening the time in purgatory was to obtain indulgences, the remission of all or part of the temporal punishment owed for sins after guilt was already forgiven. By the fifteenth century, indulgences were being sold outright. In 1515, Pope Leo X authorized the sale of indulgences in Germany, ostensibly to finance St. Peter's Basilica. This abuse of the doctrine of indulgences forced Martin Luther to post his Ninety-Five Theses on the church door in Wittenberg on October 31, 1517. This challenge to an academic debate triggered the Protestant Reformation.

6 Quoted in Heinrich Boehmer, *Martin Luther: Road to Reformation* (Cleveland: The World Publishing Co., 1957), 366.

Key Events

1476	Pope Sixtus IV extended indulgences to include those souls in purgatory.
1515	Pope Leo X authorized the sale of indulgences in Germany to raise funds for the building of St. Peter's Basilica in Rome.
1517	Johann Tetzel sells indulgences not far from Wittenberg.
1517	Luther posts the *Ninety-Five Theses* on the church door in Wittenberg.

CHAPTER FOUR

The Three Treatises of 1520

The publication of the *Ninety-Five Theses* did not result in Luther's immediate excommunication. Even when the sales of indulgences dropped off dramatically by December 1517, the papacy did not take decisive action against him. Part of the reason for this was the impending death of Emperor Maximilian I, which occurred on January 3, 1519. Luther's prince and protector, Frederick the Wise, was one of the seven electors who would "elect" the next emperor. Pope Leo X hoped to have Frederick's support in his efforts to prevent Charles, Maximilian's grandson, from being chosen the next emperor. For both religious and political reasons, Frederick insisted that Luther and his ideas receive a fair hearing inside Germany. Not only was he a pious Christian who no doubt wondered if what Luther asserted was true, but he was also a prince, a subject of the emperor, who, like other princes within the Holy Roman Empire, took advantage of every opportunity to strengthen his own authority within his territory against the claims of sovereignty by both emperor and pope. Therefore, he would not allow Luther to go to Rome, where he could be expected to suffer execution as had Jan Hus at the Council of Constance in 1415. Hence, Pope Leo X had to be very cautious in his efforts to silence Luther. He did not issue a papal bull threatening Luther with excommunication until June 15, 1520. In the meantime he employed other means to reduce Luther's influence.

In mid-October 1518, Leo X granted Luther an interview in Augsburg with the papal legate, Cardinal Thomas Cajetan. Cajetan made it clear to Luther that his attack upon indulgences was an attack upon papal authority. By doing so, the cardinal helped Luther clarify his own position. Previously Luther had appealed to the Church Fathers and canon law as well as Scripture and reason. The interview with Cajetan forced Luther to rely more heavily on the authority of Scripture alone.[1] It was becoming clearer that from the perspective of the church authorities that the real issue was not indulgences, but the authority of the pope as Christ's vicar on earth to interpret Scripture. Cajetan demanded that Luther recant. Luther refused, hastily returning to the safety of Wittenberg. The cardinal then demanded that Frederick the Wise either send Luther to Rome or banish him from Electoral Saxony. To acquiesce in the cardinal's demand would have diminished Frederick the Wise's claim to sovereignty over Electoral Saxony. Hence, Frederick declined.

Between June 27 and July 16, 1519, Luther debated indulgences and papal authority with the very able defender of the papacy, Johann Eck, the distinguished professor of theology from the University of Ingolstadt. The debate that took place at the University of Leipzig proved to be one of the significant events in Luther's life. As noted earlier, during the course of the debate Luther acknowledged agreement with views held by the condemned heretic, Jan Hus. Luther asserted that councils can and have erred. The "power of the keys" said to have been given to the pope, Luther declared, have been given to all believing Christians. Furthermore, it was not necessary for the individual's salvation that he or she believe in the authority of the pope. "A simple layman armed with Scripture," concluded Luther, "is to be believed above a pope or council without it."[2] Eck retorted that Luther's opinions were "heretical, erroneous, blasphemous, presumptuous, seditious, and offensive to pious Christian ears. . . ."[3]

Both Eck and Luther felt that Eck had won the debate. Once again, the abuse of indulgences was sidestepped as the

1 See Heiko A. Oberman, *Luther: Man Between God and the Devil* (New York: Doubleday, 1992), 196–97.
2 Quoted in Roland Bainton, *Here I Stand: A Life of Martin Luther* (Nashville: Abingdon Press, 1950), 117.
3 Quoted in Ibid., 116.

issue of papal authority took center stage. The fact that Luther had openly affirmed opinions held by Hus, opinions condemned as heresy by the Council of Constance, was of more immediate importance. In effect, Luther admitted that he was a heretic.

Three publications that reached Luther in early 1520 served to prod him into writing his three most important works, the three treatises, wherein he clarified what was only hinted at in the *Ninety-Five Theses:* his new theology. The first of these was Ulrich von Hutten's (1488–1523) German edition of Lorenzo Valla's (1404–57) treatise of 1440, demonstrating that the *Donation of Constantine* was a clever eighth-century forgery. The *Donation of Constantine* is a document that claimed the Roman emperor Constantine the Great (274–337) gave sovereignty over the western Roman Empire to the bishop of Rome, the pope. Luther's study of Valla's treatise strengthened his earlier suspicion that the pope might be the "Antichrist." Luther did not actually believe that the Antichrist would be a specific person who would appear during the last days, as some theologians believe is revealed in Scripture. Instead, he believed in "a spirit of Antichrist" that could inhabit many antichrists, for example, the papacy.

In April and June 1520, copies of two polemical works by Augustine Alfeld (b. 1480) and Sylvester Mazzolini Prierias (1456–1523) reached Luther in Wittenberg. In the first, *On the Apostolic See,* Alfeld, a Franciscan friar, defended the primacy of the pope as the cornerstone of the church. Alfeld asserted that Christ had founded only one true church and had made Peter and his successors the visible head of that church. Those who refused to accept the authority of the pope could not be members of the church.

Alfeld's polemic was not well formulated nor its thesis well argued. Nevertheless, Luther had to acknowledge that it influenced even some of the professors at the University of Wittenberg. Much more serious was the polemic by Prierias, a theologian at the papal court, which Luther described as a "hellish manifesto." In *Dialogue Concerning the Power of the*

Pope, Prierias argued that "every decision of the pope in questions of faith and morals is infallible because it comes from God, and hence every such decision is to be received by everybody without opposition, under pain of temporal and eternal death."[4] Prierias concluded that since the pope is the infallible head of the church on earth, he wields more authority than either church councils or the Scriptures themselves. This idea was too much for Luther to accept. As historian Heiko A. Oberman points out, the subordination of Scripture to papal authority was for Luther "the ultimate anti-Christian perversion of the teachings of the Church."[5] Luther's response to his enemies was the three treatises published between June and November 1520.

To the Christian Nobility of the German Nation Concerning the Reform of the Christian Church (1520)[6]

To the Christian Nobility was written during June 1520, and completed on June 23, when it was sent to the printer. The first four thousand copies sold out quickly, and it was soon reprinted in Leipzig, Strasbourg, and Basel. Luther made some changes to his treatise and published a new edition in August. Elements of it appeared earlier in *Treatise on Good Works* and *On the Papacy in Rome,* both of which had appeared in May 1520. *To the Christian Nobility* differs from Luther's earlier works in that Luther meant it as a warning to the German ruling class, not an exposition of Scripture or a theological study. It is, in fact, Luther's first *political* tract.

---

4 Boehmer, *Martin Luther,* 317–18.
5 Oberman, *Luther,* 43.
6 Somewhat different titles have been given to this work in English, for example, *Address to the Christian Nobility and Open Letter to the Christian Nobility of the German Nation.* The title and translation used here is that which appears in *Luther's Works,* vol. 44, translated by Charles M. Jacobs and revised by James Atkinson (Philadelphia: Fortress Press, 1966), 115–217.

To the Christian Nobility undermines the medieval concept of human society referred to as Christendom, "Christ's
Kingdom." According to the medieval view that was still
widely held in Luther's day, all Christian nations formed a
unified whole, sometimes referred to as the church and sometimes referred to as the state. Within that society were two
estates, the spiritual and the secular. This duality was reflected
in two governing powers, priesthood and kingship, and in
two laws, ecclesiastical and secular. Opinions differed as to
whether the spiritual or secular power should have preeminence, or whether the spiritual should have preeminence in
spiritual affairs, while deferring to the secular in secular matters, or vice versa.[7] Luther undermined the medieval view of
society by removing the distinction between the spiritual and
the secular estate.

To the Christian Nobility may be divided into three sec-
tions. In the first section Luther demolished the "three walls"
which the Romanists (supporters of the papacy) erected to
protect the church position. The first wall was the claim that
"the spiritual power is above the temporal." The second wall
was the claim "that only the pope may interpret the Scriptures." The third wall was the claim that "no one may sum-
mon a council but the pope."[8]

In his assault on the first wall, Luther refers to I Corin-
thians 12:12–13 to support his assertion that "all Christians
are truly of the spiritual estate, and there is no difference
among them except that of office." Thus the pope created a
false distinction between spiritual and secular by anointing,
ordaining, and consecrating some to church offices. "He,"
[the pope], says Luther, "might well make a man into a hypo-
crite or a humbug and blockhead, but never a Christian or a
spiritual man." Again, referring to Scripture (I Peter 2:9 and
Rev. 5:9–10), Luther concluded that "all [Christians are]

---

7 On how Luther's ideas, expressed in both *To the Christian Nobility* and *The Babylonian Captivity of the Church,* threatened the whole
medieval synthesis, see Boehmer, *Martin Luther,* 317–46.
8 *Luther's Works,* vol. 44, 126.

consecrated priests through baptism." This is Luther's doctrine of the "priesthood of believers."[9]

In his assault on the second wall, the claim that only the
pope can authoritatively interpret Scripture, Luther asserted
that there was nothing in Scripture to support such an idea.
He held that the power of the keys [to heaven and hell]
(Matt. 16:19) was given to all believers, not just to Peter and
his successors. It is also written that "the keys were not ordained for doctrine or government, but only for the binding
or loosing of sin,"[10] the priest's power to forgive sin in God's
place. Appealing again to the community of believers, Luther
said that every Christian could interpret Scripture. The popes,
who had often been without faith, should listen to those
who are better able to understand and defend the true faith.

The third wall, the claim that only the pope can call or
confirm a council, Luther said "falls of itself when the first
two are down." Again, Luther pointed out that there is no
Scripture to support the papal claim. Also, if every believer is
a priest, "when necessity demands it, and the pope is an of-
fense to Christendom, the first man who is able should, as a
true member of the whole body, do what he can to bring
about a truly free council." Luther assumed that it was to be
the temporal authorities, the princes, who as "fellow-Chris-
tians, fellow-priests, fellow-members of the spiritual estate,
[and] fellow-lords over all things" would convene a council
and reform the church.[11]

In the second section of *To the Christian Nobility,* Luther
gave examples of the abuses within the church with which a
council should deal. Among these abuses were the worldly
splendor that surrounded the pope, which contrasted unfa-
vorably with the humble lifestyles of Jesus Christ or the
Apostle Peter:

9 Ibid., 127.
10 Ibid., 134.
11 Ibid., 136, 137. What Luther was proposing as a "council" was
really an assembly, or diet, of the princes (Boehmer, *Martin Luther,*
334).

It is horrible and shocking to see the head of Christendom, who boasts he is the vicar of Christ and successor of St. Peter, going about in such a worldly and ostentatious style that neither king nor emperor can equal or approach him. He claims the title "most holy" and "most spiritual," and yet he is more worldly than the world itself.[12]

Such splendor as the pope surrounds himself with was "offensive," said Luther, "and the pope [was] bound for the sake of his own salvation to set it aside."[13]

Luther also called attention to the vast papal court which he referred to as "a swarm of parasites," the likes of which were unknown even in ancient Babylon. How was such luxury financed? Luther cataloged the numerous financial abuses with which the Romanists robbed Germany. Like ravenous wolves, he held, the Romanists preyed upon the German sheep, whom they regarded as "Drunken Germans," who had no choice but to submit and pay.

In the third and final section of *To the Christian Nobility*, Luther gave a wide range of proposals for reform. These included such things as an end to *annates* (the payment to the pope of the first year's income from a church office by the newly appointed office holder), an end to the selling of indulgences, abolishing or at least reducing endowed masses for the dead, and ceasing to canonize new saints. In general, Luther wished that the pope's power and responsibilities be reduced, so that he would have more time to study the Bible. Luther did not stop with reform of the papacy and the church, making concrete recommendations for the reform of society. Begging was to be prohibited, whether by the poor or mendicant monks (who begged for their living). Luther held that everyone should be required to work, and those who could not, should be cared for by charity from the church or the community chest.

12 *Luther's Works,* vol. 44, 138.
13 Ibid., 139.

Luther also called for the reform of the universities and education in general. He believed that all education should be Bible-centered and have as its goal the production of educated lay people, as well as clergy, who could "stand in the front line against heretics, the devil, and all the world." "Every [educational] institution," said Luther, "that does not unceasingly pursue the study of God's word becomes corrupt. . . . I greatly fear that the universities, unless they teach the Holy Scriptures diligently and impress them on the young students, are wide gates to hell."14

Luther concluded *To the Christian Nobility* with the promise that there was more of his writing to come. Having assaulted the three walls behind which the pope and his supporters stood, Luther planned to attack the central stronghold, the sacramental system by which the Romanists held captive Christ's church. Luther was already working on his next major treatise, *The Babylonian Captivity of the Church.*

The Babylonian Captivity of the Church (1520)[15]

The "Babylonian Captivity" is a reference to the captivity of the Hebrews in ancient Babylon as related in the Old Testament. In this, the most radical of Luther's three treatises, he undermined the very foundation of the late medieval church, dependent as it was on the sacramental system. According to the church of Luther's day, God's grace was dispensed to the believer through a system of seven sacraments—baptism, confirmation, penance, Eucharist (Communion), extreme unction, holy orders, and matrimony. The church held a monopoly over the dispensing of the sacraments as they could only be performed by the clergy. The sacraments were believed to be efficacious regardless of the spiritual state of the priest performing them or the faith of

14 Ibid., 206–207.
15 Trans. by A. T. Steinhauser (revised by Frederick C. Ahrens and Abdel Ross Wentz), *Luther's Works,* vol. 36 (Philadelphia: Fortress Press, 1959), 3–126.

the recipients. Thus, according to Luther, Christians were taken captive by a papal tyranny through its control over the sacraments.

Luther gave his new treatise the title, *A Prelude of Martin Luther on the Babylonian Captivity of the Church,* referring to it as a "Prelude," because he intended to follow it with more detailed treatises on the sacraments.[16] *The Babylonian Captivity* was written in Latin, an indication that Luther did not intend it for ordinary people. His following works on the sacraments were written in German and meant to be read by lay people as well as theologians.

Nearly half of *The Babylonian Captivity* is devoted to a discussion of the Holy Eucharist and baptism, the only two of the seven sacraments Luther was willing to retain because they had biblical origins. There was in fact, according to Luther, only one true sacrament, the Word of God, "and three sacramental signs, baptism, penance, and the Lord's Supper."[17] After a careful examination of penance, Luther concluded that it was not a true sacrament after all, since it lacked a physical sign (e.g., water, bread, wine).

The most important conclusion of Luther's examination of the sacraments was his transformation of the Mass from a reenactment of Jesus Christ's sacrifice on the Cross, a sacra-

16 Those that followed are *The Misuse of the Mass* (1521), *Receiving Both Kinds in the Sacrament* (1522), *The Adoration of the Sacrament* (1525), *The Abomination of the Secret Mass* (1525), and *The Sacrament of the Body and Blood of Christ—Against the Fanatics* (1526). They may be found in English translation in volume 36 of *Luther's Works.*

17 Boehmer, *Martin Luther,* 322. Protestant churches often refer to Communion as the Lord's Supper. Protestants do not agree as to whether or not, or to what extent or how, Christ is present in the Communion service. According to Roman Catholic teaching, the Eucharist is the "sacrifice of Christ's body and blood." The term denotes "the real presence of Christ in the Sacrament and the Sacrifice under the appearances of bread and wine" (Robert C. Broderick, comp., *Concise Catholic Dictionary* [St. Paul: Catechetical Guild Educational Society, 1944], 131–32).

ment which imparts saving grace, into the Lord's Supper (Holy Communion), a sacrament without any sacrificial implications or bestowal of saving grace. The clergy most clearly exercised its tyranny over the laity through the sacrament of the Eucharist. According to the doctrine of transubstantiation, confirmed as dogma in 1215 by the Fourth Lateran Council, the bread and wine consecrated during the Mass become the flesh and blood of Christ, even though they appear to the senses to remain bread and wine. Therefore, each time the Mass is performed, Christ dies again upon the altar. Since this "miracle" could be performed only by an ordained priest, the church was the only custodian of the body of Christ. Therefore, the church could deny salvation to the individual by merely withholding these elements. To Luther, this was the greatest tyranny.

Luther insisted that the priest does not "make God" in the celebration of the Mass. Nor does the priest "sacrifice Christ" upon the altar. Jesus Christ said when on the cross, "It is finished" (John 19:30). Luther interpreted this to mean that the sacrifice could not be repeated in the Mass. Likewise, when Christ instituted the sacrament of the Eucharist, he said, "This is my body. . . ." (1 Cor. 11:24). Hence, Luther reasoned that Christ is present "under (or with) the species of bread and wine", although the elements remain bread and wine. This view of Christ's presence in the Eucharist held by Luther has become known as consubstantiation, and was a position held earlier by William of Ockham. Christ's presence in the elements is discerned by faith, itself a gift of God. If the gift of faith is given by God according to his sovereign will, then the sacrament of the Lord's Supper depends upon the faith of the recipient for its validity.

With Luther's new biblical interpretation of the Lord's Supper, the role of the ordained clergy as those empowered to dispense grace was effectively demolished. The true function of the clergy, according to Luther, should be the preaching of the gospel, not the offering of the Mass. Luther rejected ordination to the priesthood as a sacrament. Instead, he saw it as a rite in the church by which one from among the priesthood of believers is chosen to perform certain tasks, primarily preaching. Luther held that what the priest does can be done by any believer, if chosen by the congregation to do so, a radically new way of viewing the priesthood.

Luther's reasoning behind his interpretation of baptism as a sacrament is somewhat labored and conflicts with the logic of his interpretation of the sacrament of the Lord's Supper. Luther insists that the efficacy of the sacraments depends upon the faith of the recipient. Christ's presence in the elements, said Luther, are discerned by faith, a gift of God given according to his sovereign will. Not all are sovereignly chosen by God. The logic of this is that the church as the body of Christ is a community of believers (or the elect) only. In fact, Luther often spoke of the church (especially in his early writings) as a remnant. If Luther's understanding of the Lord's Supper pushed him in the direction of a believers' church, he was not willing to take that route.

Luther chose to stand with the Roman Catholic church and retain infant baptism. Since Luther insisted that the efficacy of the sacrament depends on the faith of the recipient, he chose to believe that an infant has faith, similar to the faith of an individual while asleep. Furthermore, says Luther, "Infants are aided by the faith of others, namely, those who bring them for baptism. . . . So through the prayer of the believing church . . . , the infant is changed, cleansed, and renewed by *inpoured* [emphasis added] faith."[18] Luther's understanding of the sacrament of baptism supported acceptance of the idea of a territorial church.

The idea of a territorial church simply meant that everyone within a given territory had to be of one faith, one church. This did not present a problem during the Middle Ages, for the concept of Christendom allowed for only one church, that is, the Roman Catholic church. Every individual (except Jews), wherever resident, was baptized at birth into the church and became a subject of Christ's Kingdom (Christendom). The continued acceptance of the territorial church, and with it infant baptism, fit well with the emergence of the territorial nation-states during the fif-

18 *Luther's Works,* vol. 36, 73.

teenth through seventeenth centuries. A unified state required a unified religious faith. Both Protestants and Roman Catholics believed that the individual must follow the
religion of the state, leave the territory, or face the possibility of death. Religious tolerance, or freedom of religion,
would be a by-product of the rise of secularism during the
Enlightenment, not the Reformation.

To what extent political considerations may have influenced Luther's acceptance of infant baptism will never be
known. Both the Swiss Reformer Huldrich Zwingli and
Luther's colleague and successor, Philip Melanchthon questioned the biblical basis for infant baptism, but accepted it
when faced with the political implications of believer's baptism. Zwingli especially, but also Luther and the Geneva
Reformer, John Calvin, and the Anglicans in England, envi-
sioned a close collaboration between the reformed church
and the state. Thus, it might be suggested that the practice
of infant baptism was continued by the mainline Protestant
churches as a compromise with political reality. Subsequently,
theological arguments developed to defend the practice.

Luther's position on the Lord's Supper and his acceptance of infant baptism appear to conflict. In the former, the
individual comes to God on the basis of his or her own faith
(admittedly a gift of God). In the latter, the faith necessary
for the validity of the sacrament is not the faith of the infant,
but rather the faith of the sponsor (individual, parents, congregation) which undergirds the infant. Thus baptism is a
kind of sociological sacrament which links the institutional
(i.e., visible) church to society. Every individual (except the
Jews) was a subject of the state and a member of the church
through baptism, regardless of personal convictions. Thus
the partnership between church and state, rejected by the
Radical Reformation (e.g., Anabaptists) who embraced the
concept of a believers' church, was natural for Roman Catholics, Lutherans, Anglicans, and the followers of John Calvin
alike.

The reaction to *The Babylonian Captivity* was swift and
unsurprising. Duke George (1471–1539) of ducal Saxony,
Frederick the Wise's cousin and one of Luther's bitterest

foes, found himself in sympathy with much of its content, but suppressed it in his land nonetheless. Jean Glapion, Emperor Charles V's confessor, said after reading it that he felt as if his whole body had been flogged from head to foot. Erasmus of Rotterdam, perhaps the most famous intellect in Europe of that time, felt that all hope for reconciliation between Luther and the papacy was now lost. Having previously supported Luther, Erasmus now became aware that their views on what was wrong with the church were radically different and irreconcilable. Henry VIII (1491–1547) of England not only ordered *The Babylonian Captivity* publically burned in London, but also wrote a brief book, *Assertion of the Seven Sacraments* (1521), denouncing Luther and defending the seven sacraments. In return, Pope Leo X announced that Henry VIII's pen had been guided by the Holy Spirit, and granted a ten-year indulgence to anyone who read it. Henry VIII himself was granted the title "Defender of the Faith" by the pope, which remains today among the titles held by the English sovereign even after the English Reformation.

The Babylonian Captivity marks Luther's final break with Rome. He was now convinced that the papacy was an institution that had developed over time under demonic influence. For Luther the struggle against the papacy was the struggle against the Antichrist. Just days after publication of *The Babylonian Captivity,* the papal bull threatening Luther with excommunication arrived in Wittenberg. But as Rome was saying farewell to Luther, Luther had already said farewell to Rome in June 1520.

The Freedom of the Christian (1520)[19]

The Freedom of the Christian was written during October 1520, and published in November along with *An Open Letter to Pope Leo X*. It appeared in both German and Latin, the

19 Trans. by W. A. Lambert (revised by Harold J. Grimm), *Luther's Works,* vol. 31, *Career of the Reformer I* (Philadelphia: Muhlenberg Press, 1957), 333–77.

Latin version being more carefully crafted. It is a brief ex-position of what it means to be a Christian; as Luther him-self said, "it contains the whole of Christian life in a brief form. . . ."[20] If one were to look among the vast quantity of Luther's writings for one short piece that best represented the spirit of Luther's faith, *The Freedom of the Christian* would be it. The theme of the treatise is how faith justifies the sinner.

Luther began by stating two seemingly contradictory propositions regarding freedom and bondage of the Chris-tian's spirit: "A Christian is a perfectly free lord of all, subject to none" [and] "A Christian is a perfectly dutiful servant of all, subject to all."[21] Although they appear to contradict one another, they were reconciled by the Apostle Paul in his first letter to the Christians in Corinth, when he wrote, "Though I am free and belong to no man, I make myself a slave to everyone, to win as many as possible" (1 Cor. 9:19 NIV). Paul, Luther asserted, took Jesus Christ as the example, or model, for the life of a Christian. Although "being in very nature God." Jesus Christ humbled himself and became a servant of fallen humanity, in order that through his sacrifi-cial death on the cross, he was able to provide a means by which God the Father reconciled condemned sinners to him-self without violating his own holiness.

From his own experience as a monk, Luther knew that all attempts to earn justification through good works or self-mortification led only to frustration. How do sinners come to the realization that salvation is a free gift of God's grace, received by faith, and that the life of a Christian is a life of faith, not works, a trust that God is whom he reveals himself to be in the Bible?

Luther's response was to argue that the Scriptures are divided into two parts, commandments and promises. The commandments (i.e., the Law contained in the Old Testa-ment) "show us what we ought to do but do not give us the power to do it." The individual who tries to keep the com-mandments soon discovers that he or she cannot keep any

20 Ibid., 343.
21 Ibid., 344.

one of them. The commandment, "You shall not covet" (Exod. 20:19), said Luther, "is a command which proves us all to be sinners, for no one can avoid coveting no matter how much he may struggle against it."[22] According to Luther's understanding, this is the intent, or function, of the commandments (i.e., the Law), that is, to teach fallen humanity that all are sinners, totally fallen, and incapable of doing any good. As it says in James 2:10, "For whoever keeps the whole law and yet stumbles at just one point is guilty of breaking all of it" (NIV). The answer to the sinner's dilemma is to turn to the second part of the Scriptures, the promises contained especially in the New Testament.

Having been "truly humbled and reduced to nothing in his own eyes" through the realization that he or she cannot keep any of the commandments, the sinner might turn to the promises of God, where faith in Jesus Christ alone is sufficient for salvation. Luther concludes: "Thus the promises of God give what the commandments of God demand and fulfil what the law prescribes so that all things may be God's alone, both the commandments and the fulfilling of the commandments. He alone commands, he alone fulfils."[23] This is what has been called Luther's "theology of the Cross." Luther holds that salvation is from first to last a work of God's grace alone. The result is freedom for the believer, freedom from having to earn salvation and freedom from having to live as a slave to strict religious codes.

Luther likened justification and the life of a Christian to marriage. One of the benefits of faith, as opposed to works, is

> that it unites the soul with Christ as a bride is united with her bridegroom. By this mystery, as the Apostle [Paul] teaches, Christ and the soul become one flesh [Eph. 5:31–32]. And if they are one flesh and there is between them a true marriage . . . it follows that everything they have they hold in common, the good as well as the evil. Accordingly the believing soul can boast of and glory in whatever Christ

22 Ibid., 348.
23 Ibid., 349.

has as though it were its own, and whatever the soul has Christ claims as his own."[24]

This "royal marriage" between Jesus Christ and the sinner is beneficial for the sinner. The "sins, death, and damnation" of the sinner (the bride) are assumed by Jesus Christ (the groom), and the "grace, life, and salvation" of Jesus Christ are bestowed upon the sinner.

For Luther the new relationship of the believer to Jesus Christ did not result in a life of ease. On the contrary, the believer became even more aware of the power of Satan, because he or she was still burdened with a human nature inherited from Adam and Eve. Even faithful Christians would still sin. Satan would tempt the believer to doubt the adequacy of his or her faith. The believer would once again feel compelled to perform good works in order "to earn" what he or she has already freely received from Christ.

Luther's emphasis on the believer's freedom from doing good works in order to be saved left him open to the charge of antinomianism, that is, asserting that since one is saved by grace through faith in Jesus Christ alone, the believer is free to sin without remorse. Luther countered that charge by asserting that believers are not free from doing good works and will do good works. It is the motivation that has changed. Rather than doing good works out of a need to earn spiritual credit with God, Luther argued that believers will do good works out of a new love for God and their neighbors. Luther's conclusion was that one who has been justified by faith in Jesus Christ no longer lives just for himself. Rather, "He lives in Christ through faith, in his neighbor through love. By faith he is caught up beyond himself into God. By Love he descends beneath himself into his neighbor."[25] Servant-hood, the example set by Jesus Christ, is the true freedom of the Christian.

24 Ibid., 351.
25 Ibid., 371.

Significance

Luther's literary output is phenomenal, numbering into the hundreds of books, treatises, pamphlets, sermons, etc. Those that have been translated into English and published as *Luther's Works* fill fifty-six volumes. None of his individual works are more significant than the three treatises published in 1520. Unlike the Geneva reformer, John Calvin, Luther never wrote a systematic theology. But the essence of Luther's theology, and the issues rediscovered by the Protestant Reformation are found clearly articulated in these three treatises. Had nothing else by Luther been published, or survived the trials of time, these would establish his significance in the history of the Christian church.

Summary

In 1520, Luther issued three treatises that became three of the most important tracts of the Protestant Reformation. It was in these three— To the Christian Nobility of the German Nation *(June 23 & August 18),* The Babylonian Captivity of the Church *(October 6), and* The Freedom of a Christian *(November 20)—that Luther clarified his new theology. The three treatises comprised only a portion of the enormous number of publications Luther produced during that pivotal year. In* To the Christian Nobility, *Luther attacked the authority of the pope, articulated his doctrine of the priesthood of believers, and called for, and made specific proposals for, a reform of the church and society. In* The Babylonian Captivity of the Church, *Luther attacked the sacramental system by which the papacy exercised control over the Christian laity. In* The Freedom of a Christian, *Luther set forth his belief that a right understanding of how one is justified by faith liberates the Christian to live a life of love and service to God and one's neighbor.*

Key Events

1520   Luther becomes convinced that the papacy is the Antichrist, and begins a period of polemical writing.

Luther publishes T*o the Christian Nobility of the German Nation* in June. A second edition is published in August.

The papal bull, *Exsurge Domine,* threatening Luther with excommunication is issued on June 15. It reaches Luther on October 10.

Luther publishes *The Babylonian Captivity of the Church* in October.

Luther publishes *The Freedom of a Christian* along with *An Open Letter to Pope Leo X* in November.

1521   The papal bull, *Decet Romannun Pontificem,* excommunicating Luther is issued on January 3.

CHAPTER FIVE

The Bondage of the Will

Martin Luther, in formulating his theology, openly acknowledged his debt to the humanists. It was they, both the Christian and secular humanists, but especially the former, who in one sense made the Reformation possible. The humanists provided the tools for reading the Scriptures in the form of Latin, Greek, and Hebrew grammars and glossaries, as well as translations of portions of the Bible in the original languages that were employed by Luther in his own biblical studies and translation of the Bible into German. It was noted earlier how Luther learned from Erasmus's Greek New Testament that Augustine of Hippo erred in rendering the Greek *dikaioun* (Latin, *justificari*) as meaning "to make righteous," rather than "to pronounce righteous."

Whereas the Renaissance humanists were characterized by their interest in the classical languages, the Christian humanists in particular pioneered in the quest for a better understanding of the Scriptures based on close examination of them in the original languages. To achieve this goal, the Christian humanists encouraged the study of the three biblical languages (Latin, Greek, and Hebrew). In the study of Hebrew, their efforts could bring them into conflict with powerful church authorities. Johannes Reuchlin, the leading German humanist of his day, was charged with heresy because of his efforts to encourage the study of Hebrew. Although he never joined the Lutheran cause, he openly defended Luther. Reuchlin's grandnephew, Philip Melanchthon, became Luther's closest associate and successor.

Luther's translation of the Bible, begun in 1521, was not the first German translation, but it was the first translation from the original languages. In addition to grammars and glossaries published by Reuchlin, Luther, as mentioned, also used Erasmus's Greek New Testament, a Hebrew translation of the Psalms published in 1516, and a Hebrew version of the Old Testament prepared by Jewish scholars in Italy. For the Apocrypha, Luther made use of a Greek translation published in Venice in 1518.[1]

The humanists and the Reformers both strongly criticized the medieval church and hoped to reform it. Both looked back to the early church as a model for reform. They disagreed, however, as to the root cause of the corruption in the church of their day, and therefore disagreed about how to reform the church. In general, the humanists blamed the problem on venality and corruption among the higher clergy. The papal curia, the bureaucracy through which the pope governed the church, was generally thought to be debased. Church doctrine, however, was believed to be sound. By removing the corrupt individuals and replacing them with well-educated, spiritual individuals, health would be restored to the church.

Martin Luther and the Reformers saw the problem and its solution in a different light. For them the problem was a corrupt doctrine caused by straying from the authority of Scripture. Their solution was to return to the Scriptures. As relations between Erasmus and Luther became strained, Erasmus wrote to Luther asking, "Why don't you cry out against bad popes rather than all popes?"[2] As a humanist, Erasmus believed that education could produce a moral person. Sinful people could be improved by education, since human beings are by nature good, and therefore perfectible.

1 This relationship between scholarship and Bible translation continued in the English translation authorized by James I (1566–1625). The translators acknowledged in their preface to the 1611 edition that they made use of commentaries and translations in Chaldee, Hebrew, Syriac, Greek, Latin, Spanish, French, Italian, and Dutch (Lawrence Cunningham and John Reich, *Culture and Values: A Survey of the Western Humanities* [New York: Holt, Rinehart and Winston, 1998], 322).
2 Quoted in Roland H. Bainton, *Erasmus of Christendom* (New York: Charles Scribner's Sons, 1969), 158.

Luther and the Reformers on the other hand believed that sin had so corrupted human nature that the individual could be saved only by God's grace.

Luther began as early as 1516 to suspect a fundamental theological difference between Erasmus and himself. He sensed that Erasmus, who admired Jerome (c. 345–c. 419), the early medieval scholar who translated the Vulgate (Latin version of the) Bible, did not fully understand the concept of God's grace. He felt that Erasmus put too much emphasis on human ability and not enough on God. But then, Luther admired Augustine, who emphasized the sovereignty of God. In his first letter to Erasmus, written in March 1519, Luther referred to Erasmus as "our ornament and our hope."[3] Luther hoped to get Erasmus to openly identify himself with Luther's cause. But that was not to be—Erasmus would defend Luther but not join him.

During the years 1517 to 1519, following Luther's *Ninety-Five Theses* and before his assault on the sacraments in *The Babylonian Captivity of the Church* (1520), Erasmus openly supported Luther, just as he had Johannes Reuchlin. But it was really the right of free inquiry that he defended. Thus he wrote letters meant for publication on behalf of Luther to Frederick the Wise, the archbishop of Mainz, Cardinal Thomas Wolsey (1475–1530) in England, and others. He was careful to point out that it was Luther the man, and not necessarily Luther's ideas that he defended. In a letter sent to Emperor Charles V, Erasmus wrote:

> I dare not judge of Luther's spirit. But if I favor him as a good man, as accused, as oppressed, this is the work of justice and humanity. If he is innocent he should not be delivered to a faction. If he is guilty he should be corrected. The detractors are condemning passages in the writings of Luther which are deemed orthodox when they occur in the writings of Augustine and Bernard.[4]

3 Quoted in Johan Huizinga, *Erasmus and the Age of Reformation* (New York: Harper & Row, 1957), 141.
4 Quoted in Bainton, *Erasmus of Christendom*, 158.

When in 1520, Leo X issued the bull *Exsurge Domine,* threatening Luther with excommunication, Erasmus questioned its authenticity calling it "appalling, breathing rather the savagery of the Mendicants than the spirit of gentle Pope Leo."[5]

After 1519, it became increasingly more difficult for Erasmus to avoid taking sides. He was, after all, the foremost scholar in Christendom, and both Luther's supporters and opponents pressured him to ally himself with them. But Erasmus clung to his moderate course. In May 1519, he wrote Luther: "Discreet moderation seems likely to bring better progress than impetuosity. It was by this that Christ subjugated the world."[6] But this was an age when people believed very passionately in the truth, as they understood it, and none more so than Martin Luther. Erasmus's efforts to remain neutral were interpreted by Luther and his supporters as proof that Erasmus did not understand Scripture nor have the courage to join in the battle against the papists, whom Luther saw as the enemies of truth. In March 1519, Luther wrote to Erasmus:

> We have chosen rather to bear your weakness and venerate the gift which God has given you. For the whole world cannot deny that the progress and flourishing state of letters, which tends to the true interpretation of the Bible, is a magnificent and excellent gift for which we ought to render thanks to God. I have never desired that you should give up or neglect your true vocation by concerning yourself with a business for which you have neither aptitude nor courage, and which is entirely outside your sphere.[7]

Luther went on to urge Erasmus to resist the pressures being exerted upon him to come out and attack Luther. If

5 Ibid., 160.
6 Quoted in Huizinga, *Erasmus and the Age of Reformation,* 144.
7 Quoted in James MacKinnon, *Luther and the Reformation,* vol. 3, *Progress of the Movement (1521–29)* (New York: Longmans, Green, and Co., 1929), 240.

Erasmus would do so, Luther would refrain from attacking him. But Erasmus was finding it increasingly difficult to play the role of a peacemaker in an age so intolerant of neutrality and of peacemakers.

Luther's opponents too recognized that Erasmus's scholarly labors had contributed to Luther's revolt. Therefore, Luther's enemies were also Erasmus's enemies. They accused Erasmus of being Luther's inspiration. Luther, they said, hatched the egg Erasmus laid. Some even believed that some of the works attributed to Luther were in fact written by Erasmus. Still, many believed that only the great Erasmus possessed the intellectual authority to take on Luther. Pope Hadrian VI (1459–1523) wrote to Erasmus asking him to lend his pen to the defense of the church. "Beloved son, you are a man of great learning," he wrote. "You are the one to refute the heresies of Martin Luther by which innumerable souls are being taken to damnation."[8] From England, Henry VIII, Thomas More (1478–1535), and Cuthbert Tunstall (1474–1559), bishop of London, joined the chorus in the Catholic camp urging Erasmus to attack Luther, as did Francis I (1494–1547) of France, the Emperor Charles V, and Duke George of Saxony. Finally, in 1524, Erasmus decided that he could no longer remain neutral. He chose the side he always said that he would choose if forced to do so. By his own account, in early 1524, he sat down and wrote *On Free Will*[9] in just five days. It was in print by August. In September he sent presentation copies to the pope and others who had urged him to attack Luther. To Henry VIII, he wrote: "The die is cast. My book *On Free Will* has seen the light. An audacious villany, as things now stand in Germany! I expect to be stoned."[10]

8 Quoted in Bainton, *Erasmus of Christendom*, 178.
9 *De libero arbitrio diatribe sive Callatio* has been variously translated as *Diatribe (or Discourse) Concerning Free Choice* and *A Disquisition upon Free Will*, but most often as *On Free Will*.
10 Quoted in MacKinnon, *Luther and the Reformation*, 242.

The Battle of Wills

When Erasmus decided to openly oppose Luther's teachings, he chose to criticize Luther's position on whether or not the individual possessed a free will. In his response, Luther thanked Erasmus for going right to the heart of the difference between them, and not wasting ink on minor issues like the papacy, indulgences, purgatory, etc. The tone of Erasmus's *On Free Will* is typically Erasmian—eloquent, peppered with irony—as one would expect from the author of *In Praise of Folly*. His argument for free will is presented with such moderation and gentleness that some scholars have interpreted it as proof that Erasmus was not personally involved with his subject.

Luther's *The Bondage of the Will*[11] is just the opposite of Erasmus's *On Free Will* in its tone and style. Luther sallies boldly forth as God's trumpeter, the proclaimer of his infallible truth, and defender of God's revelation in the Scriptures, the final authority. Perhaps disappointed that Erasmus did not join his cause or at least remain silent, and perhaps feeling somewhat betrayed, Luther lashed out at Erasmus in a bitter polemic. In more informal writings such as those that have become known as Luther's *Table Talk,* Luther referred to Erasmus as an atheist or at best a moralist. At one point he is recorded as having said of Erasmus, "I vehemently and from the very heart hate Erasmus."[12] There is evidence of neither moderation nor gentleness in *The Bondage of the Will.*

Both Erasmus and Luther felt that they were defending the truth by attacking the errors in the other's work. It is evident that each read the other's work not with the intent of understanding what the other was saying, but rather to

11 *De servo arbitrio* has been variously translated as *On the Will not Free* and *On the Enslaved Will,* but most often as *On the Bondage of the Will.* The translation used here is by Philip S. Watson and Benjamin Drewery. It appears as volume 33 of *Luther's Works* (Philadelphia: Fortress Press, 1972).

12 Marius, *Martin Luther,* 442.

detect the points at which his opponent's work could be refuted. This is unsurprising in an age of such intense ideological conflict as the Reformation, when a real interest in understanding one's opponent, even among different Protestant sects, was virtually unknown. In their debate, Erasmus "chose" to misunderstand Luther's position, while Luther "chose" to exaggerate Erasmus's position.

The real issue at debate was whether an individual's will can result in actions that might contribute to that individual's salvation. Near the end of the first part of *On Free Will,* Erasmus defined free will as "the power of the human will by which man can apply himself toward or turn himself away from the things which lead to eternal salvation."[13] In this definition, Erasmus does not include God's grace as a factor, which Luther was quick to point out, but neither does he exclude it, as Erasmus pointed out in his response to Luther's *The Bondage of the Will.* Neither did Erasmus specify whether he was referring to the individual before or after Adam and Eve's fall from grace. Thus Erasmus left himself open to Luther's charge that he denied the effects of mankind's fall from grace (e.g., the burden and impact of original sin), and believed that the fallen individual could perform acts worthy of merit leading to salvation. It is on the basis of this definition of free will in the first part of *On Free Will,* that Luther condemned Erasmus as a moralist and an advocate of "works piety." But Luther chose to ignore the balance of Erasmus's book, where Erasmus clarifies what he means by a free will.

Erasmus insisted that there can be no dispute over the existence of free will. Later, in *Hyperaspistis,* his response to Luther's *The Bondage of the Will,* Erasmus said that he regarded it as heretical to doubt the existence of free will. "This is a truth," he asserted, "which has been handed down by orthodox Christians with a great consensus, a truth which the church has clearly defined, a truth no longer to be dis-

13 Quoted in Harry J. Mc Sorley, *Luther Right or Wrong? An Ecumenical-Theological Study of Luther's Major Work, The Bondage of the Will* (New York: Newman Press, 1969), 283.

puted, but to be believed."[14] Although Erasmus affirmed free will, the free will he defended through the body of *On Free Will* was not, as Luther rightly pointed out, the free will he defined at the beginning, which did not appear to allow for the effects of original sin.

Erasmus did not deny original sin and its effects. He believed that as a result of the Fall, mankind lost the moral freedom to choose between good and evil, right and wrong, with which he was originally created, and became a slave to sin. However, as summarized by historian James MacKinnon, Erasmus's position was that, "The light of reason and the power of the will, which is derived from reason, were . . . not thereby completely extinguished, though the will was rendered inefficacious to do the good."[15] In other words, the Fall did not result in a will so totally corrupted that apart from God's grace the individual is incapable of doing any good act that could in any way be regarded as such by God, thus contributing to the individual's salvation. This of course is exactly what Luther was saying.

Erasmus agreed with Luther that the individual cannot obtain eternal salvation except by God's grace, which comes by way of faith. But he also insisted that the fact that God's law exists, and that God holds the sinner responsible for his transgressions of the law, commanding the sinner to do good, is evidence of free will. God, Erasmus insists, cannot hold one accountable for breaking a commandment unless one were free to obey it. Once sin is confessed, the will that was corrupted by sin is restored. Erasmus's view of the Fall agreed with that of Gabriel Biel's (see Chapter 2). Aided by God's grace, the individual can do good works.

Erasmus agreed with Luther that the individual sinner has no claim on God's mercy. But, he insisted that the fact is that God is merciful and chooses to treat the sinner as just, even though the sinner can do nothing that merits God's mercy. Erasmus describes this cooperation between God and

14 Quoted in Ibid., 281.
15 *Luther and the Reformation,* vol. III, 245.

the individual, what Biel might have referred to as "the habit of grace," by using the analogy of a toddler walking across the room to receive an apple. As paraphrased by Roland Bainton,

> The tot is about to tumble when a hand from behind applies a little boost. The babe recovers his balance and reaches the apple. That little boost is the grace of God. Without it man can go no farther. With it he can in a sense cooperate with God in working out his salvation.[16]

Indeed, there are many apparent inconsistencies in Erasmus's teaching on free will that leave him open to the charge of skepticism. But Erasmus insisted that he was not a skeptic with respect to either the Scriptures or the orthodox teachings of the church. Even the church has been skeptical, said Erasmus. It had taken its time deliberating over disputed issues (e.g., the Trinity, purgatory, transubstantiation) before giving an authoritative ruling on them. Once the church had defined something, Erasmus said, he followed "their decision and cease[d] to be a skeptic."[17] Of course, this willingness on Erasmus's part to bow to the authority of the church, rather than what Luther felt was the clear teaching of Scripture, was for Luther a monstrous idea. But then, Erasmus felt likewise with respect to what he believed was Luther's determinism.

From Erasmus's perspective, Luther was a determinist, because Luther believed that God by his sovereign decree, apart from anything the individual does or can do, has already determined the individual's eternal destiny, whether salvation or damnation. Erasmus believed the doctrine of predestination to be an outrageous idea. How could God be considered just if the individual was incapable of doing anything good, and all that one did was preordained by God's decree? A god who would condemn someone for doing what

16 *Erasmus of Christendom*, 188.
17 Quoted in McSorley, *Luther Right or Wrong?*, 281.

he cannot help but do and would grant saving grace to another who is no better, would be in Erasmus's view, a tyrant. Rather than make God appear to be the author of evil by upholding God's absolute power, Erasmus would uphold his justice and mercy by affirming free will and human responsibility. To Luther's cry, "Let God be God," Erasmus would respond, "Let God be Good."[18]

Luther and *The Bondage of the Will*

The doctrine of an unfree, or impotent will, is for Luther the very foundation of the Christian's faith. An individual can worship and serve God only by correctly understanding the relationship between God and himself. If the believer is ignorant of God's power and unaware of his own impotence before God, he will never be sure of his salvation, or whether salvation is even possible. Instead, like Luther in the monastery, he will be spiritually paralyzed by doubts and fruitless attempts to earn salvation, and, in the end, hate God instead of love him. "For if I am ignorant, what, how far, and how much I can do in relation to God," writes Luther, "I shall remain equally ignorant and uncertain what, how far, and how much God can do and does in relation to me."[19] Only by being able to distinguish between what are God's works in one's life and what are one's own works can the believer live the life of a Christian. If the believer does not, as Luther believed, possess a free will, then salvation and the life of a Christian is all dependent upon God's grace. This was the assertion Luther was making in *The Freedom of a Christian* (see Chapter 4).

Luther has the Christian finding comfort in God's promises and the courage to face life's trials because he is assured of God's immutable will, "by which He foresees, determines, and effects all that happens, and which excludes the assump-

18 Bainton, *Erasmus of Christendom,* 190.
19 Quoted in Ibid., 254.

tion that he foresees anything contingently."[20] Because God's will is not subject to the individual's will, but on the contrary rules the individual's will, the believer can trust God's promises and be certain of his or her salvation. The Christian believer lives by faith, not emotions or reason.

In *On Free Will* Erasmus asked what individual would seek to amend his or her life if one can act only as God has determined beforehand? Luther's response was "No one, for no one can. Only the elect will amend themselves by God's spirit. The others will perish unamended."[21] When Erasmus then asked, who will believe that God loves the sinner, if one is condemned simply by God's decree, Luther's response was as before, "No one will or can believe except the elect. . . ."[22] If such knowledge led some (those not elected to salvation) to live lives of abandon to sin, at the same time it enabled those elected to salvation to live lives of righteousness.

Borrowing an analogy from Augustine, Luther said that the individual is like a mule ridden by either God or the Devil. If by God, he can only will what is good. If the Devil is in the saddle, he can will only what is evil. God's law (e.g., in the Old Testament) exists only to demonstrate to the individual that he or she is incapable of doing good. The gospel exists to offer God's grace.

Luther refused to make a distinction between foreknowing and foreordaining as did Erasmus in *On Free Will* and as did the scholastic theologians before him. Erasmus tried to defend God's justice by not making him the author of evil. Luther insisted that divine foreknowledge involves divine foreordination. He argued that the ninth chapter of Romans makes it clear that some are punished for acting as God has willed them to act, which he admits is a hard doctrine, but God may do as he wills, and the individual can only conclude that what God wills must be right.

20 Quoted in Ibid., 254–55.
21 Quoted in Ibid., 257.
22 Quoted in Ibid.

It is difficult for Luther to escape Erasmus's charge of being a determinist. Erasmus asked, if the individual is at the mercy of an inexorable will beyond himself, then is not the individual a mere machine, or automaton bereft of either conscience or reason, incapable of morally responsible action? But like Erasmus, Luther qualified his answer in writing and in practice. Luther insisted that predestination applied only to the area of salvation, not to the matters of everyday life. There are many important areas of human activity in which God grants the individual free choice. According to Luther:

> Free choice is allowed to man only with respect to what is beneath him and not what is above him. That is to say, a man should know that with regard to his faculties and possessions he has the right to use, to do, or to leave undone, according to his own free choice, though even this is controlled by the free choice of God alone, who acts in whatever way he pleases. On the other hand in relation to God, or in matters pertaining to salvation or damnation, a man has no free choice, but is a captive subject, and slave of the will of God or the will of Satan.[23]

As a pastor before his congregation, Luther did not preach predestination, as if he agreed with Erasmus that to do so would be to encourage licentiousness among his parishioners. Instead, he exhorted them to believe (as if they have a choice) and to do good works. Such good works are of course, as he taught in *The Freedom of the Christian,* the fruit of the spirit, the love of God flowing through the Christian to his neighbor. Just months before his death in 1545, Luther preached a sermon to his congregation in Wittenberg, in which he chastised them for their sinful behavior. If good works were a sign of being among the elect, then the adulterous and selfish lifestyle of some may be evidence that baptism does not guarantee salvation.

23 Quoted in Marius, *Martin Luther,* 461.

Significance

Luther's *The Bondage of the Will* and the controversy with Erasmus that provoked him to write it is significant for at least two reasons. First because it marks the point at which the Protestant Reformation separated itself from Christian humanism. The Christian humanists also desired a reformation of the church, but differed with Luther and the other reformers as to both the cause of the corruption and the cure of it. Second, the dispute over free will points to the cause of the main division among Protestants from the time of the Reformation to the present day.

Like Luther and the other Reformers, the Christian humanists believed that the church was mired in corruption and in desperate need of reform. The Christian humanists, however, looked to education and a greater knowledge of the classics, especially the Scriptures, as the solution. Like Socrates and the early Greek humanistic philosophers, Erasmus and his colleagues believed that knowledge would drive out ignorance and with it the corruption in the church. Knowledge would create virtuous, morally good people who would take the place of the outwardly religious, but morally corrupt priests and prelates in the church. This was what Erasmus, borrowing a term from the German humanist, Rudolf Agricola (1444–85), called the "philosophy of Christ." According to the philosophy of Christ, one must take the life of Jesus Christ as one's model and seek to live a moral and ethical life.

The notion that education can produce a virtuous person was odious to Martin Luther and the Reformers. For them, knowledge of the Scriptures, even in their original languages, could not create a virtuous person. It could only lead to knowledge of one's own sinful nature and need for salvation. To try and conform one's life to the model of Jesus Christ, without God's grace, could lead only to bondage to works righteousness.

Luther's *The Bondage of the Will* and the controversy with Erasmus and Christian humanism over free will is also significant for the light it can shed on the split within Protestantism between those who believe that the individual, although fallen and corrupted by original sin, still possesses a free will, and those who do not. Although we tend to think of this division as originating in the dispute between the followers of John Calvin and Jacobus Arminius (1560–1609), Luther's *The Bondage of the Will* and Erasmus's *On Free Will* reminds us that the question of free will has been disputed throughout the history of the church.[24]

Summary

Martin Luther wrote The Bondage of the Will *during the autumn of 1525 in response to Erasmus's* On Free Will, *which appeared in late September 1524. Luther considered* The Bondage of the Will *to be among his two or three most important works. Both Luther and Erasmus agreed that their debate over the nature of human will, and the extent to which it is free or not free, touched the heart of the difference between them. The debate also goes to the very heart of the difference between Luther and the Christian humanists, and between the Protestant Reformation and the Roman Catholic church. This question of whether or not fallen humanity possesses a free will has been debated by Christians throughout the history of the church. Since the Reformation it has divided sects within Protestantism, as for example, the Calvinist and Arminian camps.*

24 On this issue see Paul R. Waibel, *Quiknotes: Christian History* (Wheaton, IL: Tyndale House, 2000), 91–92.

Key Events

1524   Desiderus Erasmus of Rotterdam publishes *On Free Will*, an attack upon Luther's teachings.

1524–25   The Peasants' Revolt occurs in Germany. The peasants appeal to Luther's writings to justify their rebellion. The peasants feel betrayed by Luther when he condemns their acts and the princes crush the rebellion.

1525   Luther marries the former Cistercian nun, Katherine von Bora on June 13. In December, Luther publishes *The Bondage of the Will* in response to Erasmus's *On Free Will*.

✦ CHAPTER SIX ✦
Against the Peasants and the Jews

Two areas of Martin Luther's life are troublesome for modern people: his failure to support the peasants during the Peasants' Revolt in 1525, and his vicious outburst against the Jews in 1543. Luther was a religious reformer, not a social reformer and very much a man of his times. He abhorred revolt in any fashion, although he, himself, launched one of the most far-reaching revolutions in history. Also, he was a staunch defender of the social hierarchy of late medieval society. Thus, when the German peasants revolted in 1525, and appealed to Luther's writings for justification, Luther struck against them with his blistering treatise, *Against the Robbing and Murdering Hordes of Peasants,* in which he called upon the princes to suppress the peasant revolt without mercy. Luther's outburst against the Jews in 1543 is even harder to understand. By 1543, Luther believed that the Last Days had begun. Although earlier in 1523, when he wrote *That Jesus Was Born a Jew,* he believed that there would be a great conversion of Jews during the Last Days, he apparently despaired of such a belief by 1543, when he wrote *On the Jews and Their Lies.* As he neared the end of his life, he realized that the Jews would not convert, and this realization, together with the appearance of the Catholic Counter Reformation, the growing belief that the Reformation seed had fallen on less than ideal soil in Germany, his declining health and frequent periods of deep depression, led to his outburst of anti-Semitism.

Many of Luther's supporters, even Philip Melanchthon, were dismayed, even horrified, by the content of *Against the Robbing and Murdering Hordes of Peasants* and *On the Jews and Their Lies.* There can be no doubt about the harm they

83

did to the cause of the Protestant Reformation and to the church ever since. However, these controversial works must be discussed in a complete and balanced picture of Martin Luther.

Luther and the Peasants

Sporadic peasant revolts were not unknown in the late Middle Ages since the peasants were a horribly oppressed class, who had little to look forward to but a short life of monotonous toil for their masters. The attitude of the ruling class towards the peasants was evident in the proverb, "Peasants and pigs are one and the same," or another that said, "Don't grieve for a peasant or a Jew."[1] The peasants spent their lives prying from the earth the wealth that allowed the lords and their ladies to enjoy a life of leisure and luxury. Despite their labor, the peasants were not allowed to hunt in the forests, fish in the streams, or even cut down a dead tree for firewood, upon pain of death or maiming. They were expected to survive off the little grain left them after the lord of the manor took the lion's share. Little wonder that from time to time, when the thin line between mere survival and starvation was crossed, the peasants, like cornered rats, rose up against their oppressors, only to be struck down again by the lords.

What made the Peasants' Revolt of 1525 different was its scope, its violence, and especially the brutality with which it was crushed by the aroused nobility. It began in June 1524, when peasants of the Count of Lupfen in the Black Forest were commanded by the countess to gather strawberries and snails during harvest time, when their own survival depended on the harvest. From there the revolt spread widely through Germany during the autumn and winter of 1524–25, but was particularly strong in Swabia, Franconia, and Thuringia. In various locations the peasants drew up lists of their grievances and demands for reform. The best known of these lists,

1 Marius, *Martin Luther,* 417.

or manifestos, was the *Twelve Articles*[2], drawn up and adopted by the peasants of Upper Swabia in March 1525. The Anabaptist leader Balthasar Hubmaier (c. 1480–1528), together with a reform-minded Lutheran pastor, helped draft the *Twelve Articles.*

The *Twelve Articles* were less radical than other lists of grievances and demands that appeared in various places, their moderate tone perhaps due to Hubmaier's influence. They renounced violence and any attempt to overthrow the existing ecclesiastical or secular authority. What they called for was a society based on the biblical principle of a Christian brotherhood. To that end the articles called for relief from the injustices arising from the arbitrary and unchristian abuse of authority by both ecclesiastical and secular princes. In sum, the *Twelve Articles* called for "congregational election of pastors, modification of tithes, abolition of serfdom, discontinuing enclosure of common lands, elimination of feudal dues, and reforming the administration of justice."[3] Martin Luther was optimistically named in some editions of the *Twelve Articles* as a possible arbiter between the peasants and the lords.

The fact that Luther was selected as a possible mediator was certain to solicit a response from him. The notion of a society based on Christian brotherhood was an alluring idea to the peasantry, easily extractable from the Bible as well as from Luther's writings. As some historians have pointed out, Luther laid the theological basis for such a society, especially in *The Freedom of a Christian.*[4] As literacy spread among the

2 A translation of the *Twelve Articles* may be found in volume 46 of *Luther's Works, The Christian in Society III,* edited by Robert C. Schultz (Philadelphia: Fortress Press, 1967), 8–16.

3 J. D. Douglas, ed., *The New International Dictionary of the Christian Church* (Grand Rapids, MI: Zondervan Publishing House, 1978), 759.

4 See, e.g., William R. Estep, *Renaissance and Reformation* (Grand Rapids: William B. Eerdmans Publishing Co., 1986), 143. *The Freedom of a Christian* is discussed in Chapter 3.

lower classes, including the peasants, they could see for themselves in the gospels how Jesus Christ identified with the poor. The peasants' identification of the cause of social and economic justice with Luther's teachings threatened to turn the Protestant princes against Lutheranism. Johann Eck, Luther's nemesis from the Leipzig debates, like other Roman Catholic leaders, quickly blamed Luther for the Peasants' Revolt. Eck was also quick to point out that the revolt divided Lutherans, turning the rich against the poor.

When Luther received a copy of the *Twelve Articles* sometime in early April 1525, his first act was to write a response while on a journey to Thuringia, one of the "hot spots" of the revolt. It was published in early May under the title, *Admonition to Peace: A Reply to the Twelve Articles of the Peasants in Swabia*.5 Luther probably wrote the *Admonition to Peace* in the desperate hope of averting certain bloodshed just over the horizon. Also, since the peasants justified their cause as a Christian one and offered to accept correction where it could be shown to be in conflict with Scripture, Luther prepared to demonstrate such a conflict.

Admonition to Peace may be divided into three parts. In the first part, Luther addressed the princes and lords, both secular and ecclesiastical. He accused them of ranting and raving against the gospel. As for their treatment of the peasants, Luther charged: "As temporal rulers you do nothing but cheat and rob the people so that you may lead a life of luxury and extravagance."6 Unable to bear their tyranny any longer, the peasants cried out for justice and threatened rebellion, and Luther saw the hand of God in these events.

Luther cautioned the princes to see God's righteous wrath and chastening of them in the events that were unfolding. God, he said, had already sent "false teachers and prophets among us, so that through our error and blasphemy we may richly deserve hell and everlasting damnation."7 According

5 Trans. by Charles M. Jacobs and Robert C. Schultz, *Luther's Works,* vol. 46, *The Christian in Society III,* 17–61.
6 Ibid., 19.
7 Ibid., 19–20.

to Luther, it might be God's will to allow the devil, by using false prophets, to stir up the peasants against their lords, but it was not the peasants so much as God himself who was opposing them. As to the peasants' protests expressed in the *Twelve Articles*, Luther called them "right and just, for rulers are not appointed to exploit their subjects for their own profit and advantage, but to be concerned about the welfare of their subjects."[8]

Having chastised their lords, Luther turned in the second part of *Admonition to Peace* to do likewise with the peasants. He admonished them not to consider their strength or the evils of princes, but whether or not they acted "justly and with a good conscience." He warned that their "eternal fate" of both "body and soul" was at stake. While reiterating that the lords were "wicked and unjust," "suppress[ed] the gospel," unjustly took property, and inflicted "intolerable injustices" on their subjects, Luther denied their subjects any remedy other than prayer,[9] not the most satisfying option for them.

Citing Scripture passages, Luther insisted that it was a sin to rebel against authority ordained by God, however evil or displeasing to God that authority may be. Only those to whom God had given the sword may use it: thus only those in authority could correct others in authority.[10] Even a child can understand, said Luther, that "the Christian law tells us not to strive against injustice, not to grasp the sword, not to protect ourselves, not to avenge ourselves, but to give up life and property, and let whoever takes it have it. . . . Suffering! suffering! Cross! cross! This and nothing else is the Christian law."[11] As to the peasants' appeal to the Scriptures to

---

8   Ibid., 23.
9   Ibid., 23, 25, 26, 32.
10 One might ask, how then could Luther "correct" the Pope? Luther, of course, was not correcting the Pope, but insisting that the Pope submit to the authority of Scripture, just as all Christians must do, including peasants and princes.
11 *Luther's Works*, vol. 46, 29.

justify their actions, Luther cited Scripture again for his blunt response: "For no matter how right you are, it is not right for a Christian to appeal to law, or to fight, but rather to suffer wrong and endure evil; and there is no other way."[12]

For Luther, the idea that the peasants would rebel against the authorities which God has placed over them, and in so doing seek to justify their rebellion with appeals to Scripture, was evidence that they had allowed themselves to be led astray by false prophets. Since they were acting against the "common, divine, and natural law which even the heathen, Turks, and Jews have to keep if there is to be any peace or order in the world,"[13] they were in fact unchristian. Should the revolt come to armed conflict, Luther claimed, it would be heathen subjects fighting against rulers who are also heathen for, "Christians do not fight for themselves with sword and musket, but with the cross and with suffering, just as Christ, our leader, does not consist in conquering and reigning, or in the use of force, but in defeat and in weakness. . . ."[14]

In the final section of *Admonition to Peace* Luther addressed both the peasants and the rulers. Neither side was Christian, he said and "nothing Christian [was] at issue" between them; both were "acting against God and are under his wrath. . . ." The lords needed to remember that both Scripture and history testify that God punishes tyrants. Likewise, the peasants should remember that they too were under the wrath of God. Even if they were to win their fight, God would send an evil spirit among them to set them against one another to their own destruction. "In short," said Luther, "God hates both tyrants and rebels: Therefore he sets them against each other, so that both parties perish shamefully, and his wrath and judgement upon the godless are fulfilled."[15] Once the fighting began he feared that Germany would be laid waste.

12 Ibid., 31.
13 Ibid., 27.
14 Ibid., 32.
15 Ibid., 40–41.

This polemic offered little hope to the peasants, and in fact, they felt abandoned by Luther. Luther hoped that war would be averted and the two classes reconciled. But, before *Admonition to Peace* was even published, southern Germany had plunged into violence, as the peasants attacked and began destroying castles, monasteries, and churches. While Luther was traveling in Thuringia, he saw the violence first hand. Fearing that the peasants aimed at nothing less than the complete overthrow of the existing social order, Luther decided to publish a second pamphlet against the spreading peasant rebellion. Just three weeks after publishing the sympathetic *Admonition to Peace*, Luther rebounded with *Against the Robbing and Murdering Hordes of Peasants,* one of the most vitriolic tracts of his entire career.

The pamphlet was written around May 14, 1525, and published sometime before the middle of the month. It is a very brief tract, a mere six pages in *Luther's Works.*[16] Luther wrote it in obvious haste after his brief trip into Thuringia. Shocked by the violence he saw, and heckled by the peasants at Nordhausen when he tried to preach against it, Luther decided on his return to Wittenberg to address the peasants more forcefully.

In *Against the Robbing and Murdering Hordes of Peasants* Luther unleashed his full fury against the peasants. He called them "mad dogs," "fatherless, perjured, lying, disobedient rascals and scoundrels," "highwaymen and murderers," and "blasphemers of God and slanderers of his holy name." He charged the peasants with committing "three terrible sins against God and man." First, they were "deliberately and violently" breaking their oath in which they swore "to be true and faithful, submissive and obedient, to their rulers." Second, they were "starting a rebellion and . . . violently robbing and plundering monasteries and castles which are not theirs." This sin is one of the worst in Luther's eyes, it was "like a great fire, which attacks and devastates a whole

16 Trans. by Charles M. Jacobs and Robert C. Schultz, *Luther's Works,* vol. 46, *The Christian in Society III,* 49–55.

land," and "makes widows and orphans and turns everything upside down." For this sin alone, said Luther, they were deserving of "death in body and soul."[17]

For Martin Luther, rebellion, which threatened to cause anarchy, and which could turn the princes against the Reformation and thus bring it to an end, was an unforgivable sin. It is here in connection with the charge of rebellion that Luther made the statement that has been quoted in history books more often than any other by him: "Therefore let everyone who can, smite, slay, and stab, secretly, or openly, remembering that nothing can be more poisonous, hurtful, or devilish than a rebel."[18] Luther accused the peasants of having allowed the devil to take possession of them, so that they would willingly do his work. The virulence of this pamphlet against the peasants leaves one wondering about Luther's mental state at the time he wrote it.

The third sin Luther charged the peasants with is that of calling themselves "Christian brethren," when "Under the outward appearance of the gospel, they honor and serve the devil, thus deserving death in body and soul ten times over."[19] The peasants, he said, were wrong to appeal to Genesis 1 and 2 as support for their claim that all were created free. In the New Testament Jesus Christ has supplanted Moses as the primary lawgiver, and Christ "subjects us, along with our bodies and our property, to the emperor and the law of this world."[20] Baptism, said Luther, "does not make men free in body and property, but in soul."[21] Luther appeared not to leave any room here for the power of the gospel to redeem society, as he felt it could redeem the sinner.

Having admonished the peasants, Luther then instructed the princes. God had given the princes the sword, and it was their duty he claimed, even if they themselves were opponents of the gospel, to use the sword to suppress the rebel-

17 Ibid., 50.
18 Ibid.
19 Ibid., 50–51.
20 Ibid., 51.
21 Ibid.

lious peasants. He reminded the Christian princes that they were the ministers and servants of God's wrath. If the prince failed to use the sword to suppress the peasants, then he was as guilty as they and in danger of forfeiting God's grace. "This is not a time to sleep," said Luther. "And there is no place for patience or mercy. This is the time of the sword, not the day of grace."[22]

The princes did not need any encouragement from Luther to suppress the rebellion. The untrained, ill-equipped and ill-led peasants, whatever their numbers, were no match for the well-trained professional soldiers with whom they eventually had to do battle. Militarily, the peasants were defeated on May 15, 1525, at the Battle of Frankenhausen in Thuringia. Eight thousand peasants faced a princely army equipped with artillery. The peasants fell before the concentrated cannon fire. When the massacre was over, five thousand peasants lay dead, but only six of their opponents fell. The peasants' leader, Thomas Müntzer, was taken captive, tortured, and eventually beheaded.

An orgy of revenge followed the Battle of Frankenhausen, as the princes went through their territories hanging, decapitating, maiming, and massacring more peasants. The brutality of some of the princes shocked even some of their fellow princes. Margrave George of Brandenburg-Ansbach wrote to his brother Margrave Cassimir, a Lutheran prince who gave free reign to his brutality, warning that such wholesale slaughter of the peasants would ultimately harm the princes themselves. "If all our peasants are done to death in this manner," wrote Margrave George, "where shall we find others to grow our food? It really behooves us to consider the matter wisely."[23] According to the lowest estimate, at least one hundred thousand peasants perished in the Peasants' Revolt and its aftermath. Thousands more sought refuge by fleeing over the border into Switzerland.

---

22 Ibid., 53.
23 Mack MacKinnon, *Luther and the Reformation,* Vol. III, 207.

It is doubtful that Luther could have prevented the slaughter of the peasants. He knew that the peasants could not possibly win against the princes, and he feared that their defeat might well mean the end of the Reformation in Germany. But presumably he could have distanced the cause of religious reformation from the peasants' demands for social and political reform without endorsing the princes' violent repression of the peasants. Out of fear for the future of religious reform, which always mattered most to Luther, he loudly proclaimed "the political nullity of the common man in a professedly Christian State," while calling for unquestioned obedience to the absolute ruler. Luther's unbalanced behavior during the Peasants' War would have tragic consequences for the course of German history through the middle of the twentieth century. Historian James MacKinnon says it well when he writes:

> . . . under the influence of the revolutionary scare, the Reformation in Germany, as directed by him [Luther], henceforth contributed to strengthen the regime of the absolute ruler, whether elector, duke, landgrave, or other petty potentate, instead of developing into the larger and more democratic movement of which it had at first seemed to be the promise, and to which his theological teaching had undoubtedly given an impulse.[24]

Luther and those who led the Lutheran movement after him (e.g., Philip Melanchthon and Martin Bucer [1491–1551]) would "dethrone an absolute pope to put in his place the absolute prince."[25] Lutheranism after 1525 ceased to be a popular movement, but instead became a tool of the princes, as Lutheranism became the German state religion.

Luther was severely criticized for his harsh words in *Against the Robbing and Murdering Hordes of Peasants.* Even his friends could not reconcile it with the earlier *Admonition*

24 Ibid., 209.
25 Ibid.

to Peace, urging him to retract his words. Common people called him "the flatterer of the princes,"[26] and Roman Catholics blamed him for having stirred up the rebellion and then abandoning the peasants, when he feared for his own life. Many rushed to point out the obvious contradictions in his published works. Finally, in July 1525, Luther answered his critics with *An Open Letter on the Harsh Book Against the Peasants.*[27]

An Open Letter was composed in early July and distributed by August 1, 1525. In it Luther made no concessions to his critics insisting that the peasants deserved death for rebelling against the authorities God had placed over them. "A rebel," wrote Luther, " is not worth rational arguments, for he does not accept them." For them there is only the "fist," the "musket ball," and the headsman, who "comes with his axe."[28]

Incredibly Luther was unforgiving in response to those, both friend and foe alike, who were so bold as to criticize him. Luther wrote that those who criticized the harshness in *Against the Robbing and Murdering Hordes of Peasants* were "certainly rebels at heart." Those who sympathized with the peasants, or who called for mercy on them, deserved the same fate—to die without mercy. If Luther's harsh stand against the peasants seems paradoxical, it is even more difficult to fathom his changing attitude towards the Jews, especially his tract, *On the Jews and Their Lies.*

Luther and the Jews

Martin Luther devoted two major treatises to the topic of the Jews. The first, *That Jesus Was Born a Jew,* published in 1523,[29] was sympathetic to them, even generous in its

26 Quoted in *Luther's Works,* vol. 46, 60.
27 Trans. by Charles M. Jacobs and Robert C. Schultz, *Luther's Works,* vol. 46, *The Christian in Society III,* 63–66.
28 Ibid., 65–66.
29 Trans. by Walther I. Brandt, *Luther's Works,* vol. 45, *The Christian in Society II,* 195–229.

language. Luther obviously hoped that it would contribute to their conversion. The later treatise, *On the Jews and Their Lies,* published in 1543, is altogether different,[30] and surpassed, if that is possible, the hateful, vindictive tone of *Against the Robbing and Murdering Hordes of Peasants.* By 1543, Luther had obviously given up all hope of the Jews converting, so he was prepared to assign them, along with the papacy, to the eternal flames.

The reason for Luther's writing *That Jesus Was Born a Jew* stemmed from charges made by some who were attending the Diet of Nuremberg in 1523. The charges, or more accurately rumors, alleged that Luther denied the belief that Jesus Christ was born of a virgin. Such a charge was as much as saying that Luther was not a Christian, for the belief that Jesus Christ was the virgin-born Messiah prophesied in the Old Testament and testified to in the New Testament, was a defining doctrine of the Christian religion. It was affirmed in the early creeds (e.g., the Apostles' Creed and the Nicene Creed) and was declared as orthodox by the early church councils. At first Luther was willing to ignore what he considered an absurd charge, but when he learned that even the emperor's brother, Archduke Ferdinand, believed the rumor and publically acknowledged it, he decided to address it and the Jews, also.[31] While confirming his adherence to the doctrine of the virgin birth, he hoped to convince the Jews that Jesus Christ was also the promised Messiah of the Old Testament.

In the opening of the treatise, Luther explained that he was only reluctantly responding to the vicious lie that was circulating which accused him of denying the virgin birth of Jesus Christ. However, since he had been persuaded to do so, he wished at the same time to write something useful.

30 Trans. by Martin H. Bertram, Ibid., vol. 47, 121–306.
31 One tactic employed by early, first century, Jewish authorities to combat the spread of Christianity was to deny that Jesus was born of the virgin Mary. Often the title given to Jesus in the Talmud is Jesus Ben-Pantera, meaning "Jesus the son of Pantera." Pantera was allegedly a Roman legionaire.

"Therefore," wrote Luther, "I will cite from Scripture the reasons that move me to believe that Christ was a Jew born of a virgin, that I might perhaps also win some Jews to the Christian faith."[32]

Luther believed that the ongoing persecution of the Jews and the fact that what had passed for Christianity was the "distorted papal and monkish form of it" were both obstacles to the conversion of the Jews. He stated that he had been informed by "pious converted Jews" that if they had not encountered the true Christian faith as rediscovered by the Reformation, "they would have remained Jews under the cloak of Christianity for the rest of their days." Luther was alluding to the fact that many Jews had converted to Christianity, but only outwardly and culturally, so as to open doors of opportunity otherwise closed and to avoid persecution or even death. Indeed, Luther claimed that if he were himself a Jew, and the only example of Christianity he knew was that of the Roman Catholic church, he "would sooner have become a hog than a Christian."[33]

Luther pointed out that Gentile Christians (i.e., non-Jewish) had no cause to be proud. The Jews were "of the lineage of Christ . . . blood relatives, cousins, and brothers of our Lord," whereas Gentile Christians were "aliens and in-laws." God had never honored the Gentiles by raising up from among them, as he had from among the Jews, patriarchs, prophets, or apostles. In fact, said Luther, there were very few genuine Christians among the Gentiles. Therefore, Luther was not afraid to identify himself with the Jews, and called upon his Roman Catholic enemies to so honor him, if they wished: "Accordingly, I beg my dear papists, should they be growing weary of denouncing me as a heretic, to seize the opportunity of denouncing me as a Jew."[34]

Luther closed *That Jesus Was Born a Jew* with an appeal to Christians to change their policies towards the Jews. In-

32 *Luther's Works,* vol. 45, 200.
33 Ibid.
34 Ibid., 201.

stead of using persecution, force, and slander, he advised Christians to "deal gently with them and instruct them from Scripture." Christians were to look to the "law of Christian love" as a guide. "We must receive them cordially," wrote Luther, "and permit them to trade and work with us, that they may have occasion and opportunity to associate with us, hear our Christian teaching, and witness our Christian life." By such means some may come to Christ, while no doubt some will prove stiff-necked and refuse. But, "After all," concluded Luther, "we ourselves are not all good Christians either."[35]

This gentle, temperate, conciliatory attitude of *That Jesus Was Born a Jew* is out of tune with the common attitude of Christians towards Jews during Luther's day, and contrasts so sharply with the harsh tone of *On the Jews and Their Lies.* One explanation for the difference is that in 1523, Luther possessed a genuine sympathy for the Jews, and a belief that if they were presented with the true Christian gospel in a spirit of Christian love, many would be converted. Some scholars believe that ample evidence exists in Luther's writings (e.g., his lectures on Romans) that he held to the belief that in the Last Days the Jews would become Christians.[36] His belief in the conversion of the Jews increased as he became convinced that the Roman Catholic church would not reform. Luther also believed that he was living in the Last Days. The time seemed right, when he wrote *That Jesus Was Born a Jew* in 1523, for evangelizing the Jews by reasoned presentation of the true Christian religion and visible acts of Christian love.

There is some evidence that Luther's position towards the Jews was basically consistent from the time when he was a young professor lecturing on the Psalms between 1513 and 1515 to the last sermon he preached on February 15, 1546, to which he appended an "Admonition Against the

35 Ibid., 229.
36 See, e.g., Richard Marius' recent biography, *Martin Luther: The Christian Between God and Death,* 375–77.

Jews."37 The noted Luther scholar Heiko A. Oberman argues that Luther's tolerance of the Jews was always a tolerance for the purpose of converting the Jews to Christianity. He did not advocate permitting the Jews to live within Christendom as practicing Jews. As Luther in his old age became more and more convinced that the terrors of the Last Days had been unleashed, and that the Last Judgment was imminent, he saw the Jews as members of a triumvirate of shock troops employed against Christendom by the Antichrist. The other two members of the triumvirate were the Turks (i.e., Muslims) and the papists. "As Luther neared the end of his days on earth," concludes Oberman, "the issue was not a Turkish crusade, or hatred of Rome or the Jews, it was upholding the Gospel against all enemies in the confusion of the Last Days."38 *On the Jews and Their Lies* was not a call for the mob to rise up in a pogrom against the Jews, but a call to arms to the princes to defend the Christian church from its enemies.

Luther apparently intended to write something about the Jews in 1538. He indicated such at the conclusion of *Against the Sabbatarians: Letter to a Good Friend,* an open letter to his friend Count Wolfgang Schlick zu Falkenau published in early March 1538. Apparently, soon after 1538, he changed his mind and resolved, as he says in the opening line of *On the Jews and Their Lies,* "to write no more either about the Jews or against them." In May 1542, Luther changed his mind again, after receiving from Count Schlick zu Falkenau a Jewish pamphlet along with a request that he refute it. Luther's response to this was *On the Jews and Their Lies,* which appeared in early January 1543.

On the Jews and Their Lies may be divided into four major parts. In the first, approximately one-fourth of the whole, Luther argued that the Jewish religion is fundamentally a "works-righteousness" religion. In the second part, roughly one-half of the total, is an exegesis of key Old Testament

37 This explanation is presented Oberman, *Luther,* 292–97.
38 Ibid., 296.

passages Luther believed were messianic, that is, spoke of the coming of promised Messiah, Jesus Christ. But in the third and fourth parts, together one-fourth of the total, Luther unleashes his full fury and wrath against the Jews. In part three, he repeats the rumors regarding the Jews that were commonly believed during the late Middle Ages. He notes that Jews have been condemned to death, having been "accused of poisoning water and wells, of kidnaping children, of piercing them through with an awl, of hacking them in pieces, and in that way secretly cooling their wrath with the blood of Christians. . . ."[39]

The fourth part of the treatise gives the whole its notoriety and is often quoted in anti-Semitic literature. There Luther addressed both the secular and ecclesiastical authorities, and made his recommendations on how to deal with the Jews. "With prayer and the fear of God," Luther called upon the authorities to "practice a sharp mercy to see whether we might save at least a few from the glowing flames."[40] Luther advised the authorities to take action on seven fronts. Here they are in Luther's own words.

> First, to set fire to their synagogues or schools and to bury and cover with dirt whatever will not burn, so that no man will ever again see a stone or cinder of them.[41]
>
> Second, I advise that their houses also be razed and destroyed. For they pursue in them the same aims as in their synagogues. . . . Instead they might be lodged under a roof or in a barn, like the gypsies.[42]
>
> Third, I advise that all their prayer books and Talmudic writings, in which such idolatry, lies, cursing, and blasphemy are taught, be taken from them.[43]

39 *Luther's Works,* vol. 47, 264.
40 Ibid., 268.
41 Ibid.
42 Ibid., 269.
43 Ibid.

Fourth, I advise that their rabbis be forbidden to teach henceforth on pain of loss of life and limb.[44]

Fifth, I advise that safe-conduct on the highways be abolished completely for the Jews.[45]

Sixth, I advise that usury be prohibited to them, and that all cash and treasure of silver and gold be taken from them and put aside for safekeeping. . . . Whenever a Jew is sincerely converted, he should be handed one hundred, two hundred, or three hundred florins, as personal circumstances may suggest. With this he could set himself up in some occupation for the support of his poor wife and children, and the maintenance of the old and feeble.[46]

Seventh, I recommend putting a flail, an ax, a hoe, a spade, a distaff, or a spindle into the hands of young, strong Jews and Jewesses and letting them earn their bread in the sweat of their brow, as was imposed on the children of Adam.[47]

Finally, Luther advised that if the Germans feared that the Jews might harm their families or their livestock, then they should follow the example of other nations of Europe and "eject them forever from the country."[48]

When Rabbi Josel von Rosheim (1478–1554), the acknowledged leader of the Jews within the Holy Roman Empire, read *On the Jews and Their Lies*, he commented: "Never before has a Gelehrter, a scholar, advocated such tyrannical and outrageous treatment of our poor people."[49] Rabbi Rosheim made the comment in a petition to the authorities in Strassburg, asking that they prohibit circulation of the treatise in Strassburg. Earlier, in 1537, the rabbi had

44 Ibid.
45 Ibid., 270.
46 Ibid.
47 Ibid., 272.
48 Ibid.
49 Quoted by the editor, Franklin Shermon, in the "Introduction" to Ibid., 135.

written to Luther asking his assistance in obtaining an audience with Elector John Frederick I (1472–1553) of Saxony. The elector had ordered the Jews out of his territory, and Rabbi Rosheim wished to persuade him to cancel his decree. Despite help from the well-known Strassburg specialist in Hebrew studies and reformer, Wolfgang Capito (1478–1541), Luther refused Rabbi Rosheim's request.

Fortunately, Luther's advice was not followed. In Electoral Saxony, Luther's prince John Frederick, who did not expel the Jews from his territories in 1537, placed certain restrictions on the Jews in Saxony. Likewise, Philip of Hesse forbade the Jews in Hesse to lend money and required them to attend Christian services. Others, as for example Elector Joachim II (1505–71) of Brandenburg, chose to follow a tolerant policy towards the Jews. In fact, there is no recorded case where Luther's advice to burn the synagogues, etc., was followed. This was in sharp contrast to how the princes responded to *Against the Robbing and Murdering Hordes of Peasants*. In fact, the treatise itself did not sell well. Its impact would await a darker era in Germany's history.

Assessment

While Luther's unbalanced position in the Peasants' Revolt and his vicious attack on the Jews in 1543 are hard to fathom, we must remember that Luther lived at the end of the Middle Ages, and so held a totally different mindset from the modern world. Like others of his era, he could not conceive of a world without a clearly defined class structure. As mentioned, the concepts of equality and tolerance among people are a by-product of the eighteenth-century Enlightenment, not the Reformation. Luther was a defender of the social and economic structure of late medieval society. He sought only a reformation of the church, not of society. He failed to understand, as did the Anabaptists and others of the Radical Reformation, that true religious revival brings with it a concern for social and economic justice as well.

Luther's outburst against the Jews in 1543 is similarly understood as being very much in line with popularly accepted opinion in the late Middle Ages, though it is perplexing to find that feeling held by one of Luther's stature and knowledge of the Scriptures. As for the vulgarity of his language in *On the Jews and Their Lies*, Luther was well known for his using such language. Despite his learning, he was from his roots, a peasant who frequently spoke and wrote in the common tongue.

In 1541, when he was fifty-seven years old, Luther's health seriously declined. A recurring ulcer on one of his legs reopened, causing him much pain. He was troubled by throat and ear infections, kidney stones, heart problems, and digestive disorders. On September 20, 1542, his beloved daughter Magdelena had died in his arms at age thirteen, casting Luther into an extended period of deep depression. During the winter, the plague struck Wittenberg, killing many of its citizens. The papacy, since 1534 under Pope Paul III (1534–49) was showing signs of renewed strength and about to launch the Catholic Counter Reformation. Germany, led by Charles V, was at war with Roman Catholic France, which was allied with the Turks (Muslims). To Luther it seemed that his beloved Germans were successfully resisting the true Christian gospel. He believed that the Last Days had begun. This was the climate in which Luther wrote his controversial pieces, sullying his image in the eyes of his followers. Finally though, these missteps do not override his great influence on the Reformation.

Summary

In his later years, troubled by ill health and depression, Luther wrote two controversial treatises, Against the Robbing and Murdering Hordes of Peasants *and* On the Jews and Their Lies. *He did not support the peasants in their rebellion of 1525 when they looked to him and his writings for help. After the massacre of the peasants by their lords in putting down the rebellion, many looked at Luther as a betrayer and returned to Roman Catholicism. Convinced that the Last Days had come, Luther wrote a vitriolic treatise against the Jews whom he had despaired of converting. In the climate of the times, Luther feared for himself and for the fate of the Lutheran Reformation in Germany. Later, his text would be quoted by anti-Semites.*

Key Events

1523   Luther writes *That Jesus Was Born a Jew* with a
        sympathetic appeal to the Jews for their salvation.

1524   The Peasants' Revolt breaks out and spreads through
        Germany during the winter of 1524–25.

1525   Luther publishes *Admonition to Peace* in early May,
        followed three weeks later by *Against the Robbing and
        Murdering Hordes of Peasants,* a harsh condemnation of
        the peasants.

1543   Luther publishes *On the Jews and Their Lies,* a vicious
        attack on the Jews in which he calls upon the princes to
        apply a policy of "sharp mercy" towards the Jews.

Martin Luther: An Assessment

Martin Luther was one of the few who walks out on to the historical stage to briefly dominate the drama and then leaves the audience forever inspired and troubled by the echo of his words. Luther, himself, once wrote that from time to time in history, God "provides a healthy hero or a wondrous man in whose hand all things improve or at least fare better than is written in any [history] book."[1] Luther was not speaking of himself, but rather of the role of great men and women in history. In the confession he is believed to have made shortly before his death, he said of his own works, "I am fully conscious and certain that I have taught correctly from the Word of God, according to the service to which God pressed me against my will; I have taught correctly about faith, love, the cross and the sacraments."[2] The only recognition Luther yearned for was to hear the words of his master: "Well done, good and faithful servant" (Matt. 25:21a).

Luther's view of history was clearly biblical. He believed that what may appear to some as a simple cause-and-effect sequence, or to others as random events, was in fact a war between divine and satanic powers. But it is not a struggle between equal powers, as in some Eastern concept of yin and yang. From a biblical perspective, history is a conspiracy within a conspiracy: God had a plan and within it, though subject to God's sovereign control, is a conspiracy, that of Satan. Satan was first in rebellion against God, and sought to

1 Quoted in *Luther's Works,* vol. 34, *Career of the Reformer IV,* edited by Lewis W. Spitz (Philadelphia: Muhlenberg Press, 1960), 271.
2 Quoted in Oberman, *Luther: Man Between God and the Devil,* 322.

draw fallen humanity into his rebellion, not that he might actually succeed, for he was defeated by Christ's sacrificial death and resurrection, but that as many as he might recruit should suffer his ultimate fate.

Luther believed in the sixteenth century what many Christians before and since have believed, that all Christians, not just clergy or the theologian, have a divine calling to serve God's will. The homemaker, as much as the woman who goes to the foreign-mission field, the farmer or the factory worker, as well as the pastor or the seminary professor, has a divine call to serve, and by so doing, join the struggle "against the rulers, against the authorities, against the powers of this dark world and against the spiritual forces of evil in the heavenly realms" (Eph. 6:12, NIV).

Luther drew strength from his conviction that he was only an instrument in the hands of a God whose presence permeated and sovereignly directed the course of history. There were times when he would doubt his own faith. These periods came when Luther was experiencing severe physical or mental suffering. From 1527 on, he endured nearly constant physical pain.

For Luther, suffering was an important part of the struggle against Satan. He did not shun the use of medicine, such as it was in his day. Medical remedies and a healthy diet were instruments to be employed in the struggle against Satan. Nor did he try to hide the physical pain or the emotional struggles from those around him. Suffering was, he believed, God's way of calling him to prayer. After one particular illness during which he feared for his life, Luther wrote to his close friend, Georg Spalatin: "I am writing you this not to evoke your pity, but so that you can congratulate me. . . . By this misery I am incited to prayer, which is what we need most: to do battle with Satan by praying with all our might."[3]

Luther drew strength from his fear of God, not the fear of a monk who knows God only as a wrathful judge, but the

---

[3] Quoted in Ibid., 328. I am indebted to Heiko A Oberman for directing me to these thoughts.

fear that means awe of God's majesty. Such fear drives away human fears and replaces them with a courage that comes from living by faith. For Luther living by faith meant trusting in God's mercy. Heiko A. Oberman puts it well when, considering the interplay between faith and fear in Luther's life, he observes that, "Faith and fear of the Lord are not mutually exclusive, but faith lives on trust in God's mercy and not the knowledge of His majesty. The faithful creep under the cross of Christ like chicks under the wings of the mother hen."[4]

By looking to the life of Jesus as an example to be followed, Luther found the spiritual strength and the courage to face whatever lay before him in his spiritual struggle. Luther believed that he as a Christian was called not only to stand against the forces of evil, but also to stand between the people and God's just wrath. In March 1522, Luther left the safety of Wartburg Castle and returned to Wittenberg against the expressed wishes of his prince and protector, Frederick the Wise. In justifying his disobedience, Luther cited Ezekiel 22:30: "I looked for a man among them who would build up the wall and stand before me in the gap on behalf of the land so I would not have to destroy it. . . ." Luther believed it his duty to erect a wall of faith between God's wrath and the people, who in Luther's absence were using their new found freedom as license to destroy the images, paintings, and stained glass windows in the churches.

Although Luther lived in the firm conviction of being an instrument of God's will, he was not perfect. Like many in history who have had moments of greatness, Luther remained a flawed man. Luther felt he must answer a struggle within the church and within himself.

Perhaps the best description of Martin Luther was written some fifty years before Luther's appearance at the Diet of Worms by another monk, known as Thomas à Kempis (c.1380–1471). In *The Imitation of Christ,* which over the intervening centuries since its first printing in 1471, has ap-

4 Ibid., 315.

peared in thousands of editions, and remains one of the most popular Christian books ever written, Thomas writes:

> Jesus has many lovers of his heavenly kingdom these days, but few of them carry the cross. He has many who desire comfort, but few who desire affliction. He has many friends to share his meals, but few to share his fasts. Everyone is eager to rejoice with him, but few are willing to endure anything for him. Many follow Jesus up to the breaking of the bread, but few as far as drinking from the chalice of his Passion. Many admire his miracles, but few pursue the shame of the cross. Many love Jesus as long as no difficulties touch them. Many praise and bless him as long as they receive comfort from him. But if Jesus hides himself and leaves them awhile, they either complain or fall into a deep depression.
>
> Those who love Jesus for himself and not for their own comfort bless him in every trial and heartfelt anguish, just as they do in moments of great comfort. And even if he should never give them comfort, they would still always praise him and always want to thank him. Oh, how powerful is a pure love of Jesus, untainted by self-interest or self-love.[5]

Perhaps what makes Martin Luther's life and work so interesting and relevant for today is the insight it gives us into the perennial search for truth and meaning. From time to time throughout history, great men and women—philosophers, mystics, religious thinkers, and artists—have asked if there is in fact an ultimate truth, and if so, how that truth can be known, if in fact it can be known.

For the humanist, the ultimate reality is impersonal matter, which has always existed. For the humanist, there is no ultimate truth, only truths, originating in the thought and experience of human beings, no one of which is anymore

5 Thomas à Kempis, *The Imitation of Christ: A Timeless Classic for Contemporary Readers,* trans. by William C. Creasy (Notre Dame, IN: Ave Maria Press, 1989), 77.

valid than another. Ultimately, all is meaningless. This is where autonomous reason has led modern thinkers at the beginning of the twenty-first century.

Individuals of religious faith hold to the belief that the ultimate reality is a personal infinite God, who exists independent of, and is the creator of, the material universe. For believers, Truth, that is, ultimate truth, does exist and originates in the creator—God. Martin Luther, and Christian believers of his day, whether Roman Catholic, Greek Orthodox, or followers of the Protestant Reformation, believed that God had made himself known in the Old and New Testament Scriptures (i.e., the Bible). The Roman Catholics believed that the church, ultimately the pope, was entrusted with the authority to interpret the Scriptures. Therefore there were two pillars of authority, the Scriptures and church tradition (decisions of church councils, papal decrees, etc.).

For Martin Luther and the Protestant Reformers, the Bible alone was the sole authority in all matters of religious faith and practice. This was what Luther asserted in his defiant stand at the Diet of Worms in 1521. The Reformation was not a struggle between various truths, or ideas, but really a struggle over who correctly understood and taught "the Truth." Since the eternal destiny of human beings depended on knowing the Truth, individuals on both sides were willing to die, even kill, to defend the truth as they understood it.

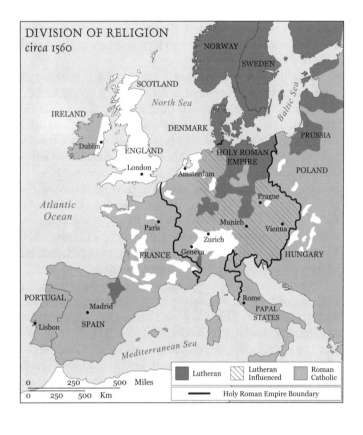

DIVISION OF RELIGION
circa 1560

NORWAY

SWEDEN

SCOTLAND

North Sea

IRELAND

DENMARK

PRUSSIA

Dublin

ENGLAND

HOLY ROMAN
EMPIRE

POLAND

London

Amsterdam

Prague

*Atlantic
Ocean*

Paris

Munich

Vienna

Zurich

FRANCE

Geneva

HUNGARY

PORTUGAL

Madrid

Rome

PAPAL
STATES

Lisbon

SPAIN

Mediterranean Sea

Baltic Sea

| | Lutheran | | Lutheran Influenced | | Roman Catholic |

0   250   500   Miles

0   250   500   Km

—————   Holy Roman Empire Boundary

Annotated Chronology of Luther's Reformation Writings

Martin Luther produced an immense literary output. Not only did he translate the entire Bible into Latin, but between 1516 and 1546, he averaged one or two treatises per month. The "official" German language edition of Luther's collected works fill sixty-seven hefty volumes.[1] A significant portion of *Luther's Works*, those deemed important to the [Protestant] Christian church, have been translated into English and published under the general title of *Luther's Works*.[2] The first thirty volumes consist of lectures on various books of the Bible, both Old and New Testaments. There are an additional five volumes of letters and sermons, a volume of hymns and liturgy, and one of informal selections known as Luther's *Table Talk*. The latter is a collection of comments Luther made at meals, which were taken down by various individuals who shared meals with the Luthers. The individual wishing to catch a glimpse of Luther, the man, should spend time reading the *Table Talk*.

The remaining eighteen volumes contain what are referred to as Luther's Reformation writings and are grouped together under such subject headings as "Career of the Reformer," "The Christian in Society," etc. These more than one hundred publications of various length are listed below in the chronological order in which they were first published, together with a line or two describing their content. The

1 D. Martin, *Luthers Werke,* 67 vols. (Weimar: Hermann Bohlaus Nachfolger, 1883–1997).
2 *Luther's Works,* eds. Jaroslav Pelikan and Helmut T. Lehman, 55 vols. (St. Louis: Concordia House; Philadelphia: Fortress Press, 1955–86).

number of the volume in which the work appears is provided in parentheses following the title. This constitutes a guide for those who wish to sample *Luther's Works*, or who wish to seek out a work on a particular topic. *Luther's Works* should be easy to find at any well-stocked college, university, or public library.

1517   *Disputation Against Scholastic Theology* (v. 31)
         Luther deals with such issues as free will, sin, and grace in this attempt to undermine the philosophy of Aristotle (384–322 BC). Aristotle's philosophy was the basis for medieval scholasticism, which was in turn the basis for the medieval view of salvation.

         Ninety-Five Theses (v. 31)
         Luther's questioning of indulgences that launched the Protestant Reformation. See Chapter 3.

1518   *Proceedings at Augsburg* (v. 31)
         Luther gives his account of the interview with Cardinal Cajetan in Augsburg during the summer of 1518. He gives the charges made against him and his answers to those charges.

         Explanations of the Disputation Concerning the Value of Indulgences [or *Explanations of the Ninety-Five Theses*] (v. 31)
         Luther applies his new "Theology of the Cross" in this explanation of his *Ninety-Five Theses*. In doing so, he questions the primacy of the pope and calls for a reformation of the church.

         Heidelberg Disputation (v. 31)
         This work contains twenty-eight theological and twelve philosophical theses, together with their proofs, presented to a meeting of the German Augustinians in Heidelberg on April 26, 1518. The question of free will is discussed in the lengthy explanation of Thesis # 6: "Is the will of man outside the state of grace free or rather in bondage and captive?"

Preface to the Complete Edition of a German Theology
(v. 31)
After reading a little book by an unknown German
mystic, Luther published it along with a brief
introduction, in which he noted that, "no book except
the Bible and St. Augustine has come to my attention
from which I have learned more about God, Christ,
man, and all things."

1519 *A Sermon on the Estate of Marriage* (v. 44)
Luther speaks of marriage as a gift from God, a cov-
enant of spiritual and physical fidelity between husband
and wife, in which the partners should seek to meet the
needs of the other, rather than their own gratification.

A Meditation on Christ's Passion (v. 42)
Luther presents pastoral counseling on the proper way
for Christians to meditate on Christ's suffering on the
Cross during the Easter season.

An Exposition of the Lord's Prayer for Simple Laymen
(v. 42)
A verse by verse interpretation of the Lord's Prayer is
given by Luther, along with a discussion of prayer in
general, all in terms that a simple lay person can
understand.

On Rogationtide Prayer and Procession (v. 42)
Luther uses the observance of Rogation days (the three
days before Ascension Day) of prayer and fasting for a
good harvest as the starting point for this sermon on
prayer. Luther says that the individual must pray relying
upon God's promises and not attempt to force God to
conform to one's own expectations.

A Sermon on Preparing to Die (v. 42)
In this sermon, Luther deals with one of the great fears
of people in the Middle Ages, the fear of death. He
asserts that those who put their trust by faith in Jesus
Christ will discover that Christ's death will overcome
their fear of death.

1519
(cont'd.)

The Sacrament of Penance (v. 35)
In this first of three sermons on the sacraments delivered in 1519, Luther is still holding to penance as a sacrament, along with baptism and the Lord's Supper. In 1520, he reduced the sacraments to two, baptism and the Lord's Supper.

The Holy and Blessed Sacrament of Baptism (v. 35)
In his second sermon on the sacraments, Luther distinguishes three parts in the sacrament of baptism— the sign, what the sign signifies, and faith.

The Blessed Sacrament of the Holy and True Body of Christ, and the Brotherhoods (v. 35)
In this third sermon on the sacraments delivered in 1519, Luther sees three parts to the sacrament of the Lord's Supper—an outward sign, an inward significance, and a living faith. He also proposes giving both elements (bread and wine) to the laity.

The Leipzig Debate (v. 31)
The famous debate between Luther and Johann Eck at Leipzig in 1519 made reconciliation between Luther and the Roman Catholic church impossible. Luther presents his letter to his colleague, George Spalatin, describing the debate, together with the thirteen theses he defended.

Two Kinds of Righteousness (v. 31)
In this sermon preached, it is believed, on Palm Sunday in 1519, Luther applies his doctrine of salvation by faith to everyday life. He distinguishes between Christ's righteousness and the righteousness of the believer, which is made possible by Christ's righteousness.

1520

Treatise on Good Works (v. 44)
Luther explains how good works rest upon, and proceed from, the supreme good work, which is faith in Jesus Christ.

*To the Christian Nobility of the German Nation
Concerning the Reform of the Christian Estate* (v. 44)
This is one of the three treatises of 1520 in which
Luther presents the basic doctrines of the Reformation.
Here Luther attacks the three walls behind which the
papacy hides, holding authority over Christians. See
Chapter 4.

Fourteen Consolations (v. 42)
Originally written to comfort Frederick the Wise,
Luther's prince, who became ill in 1519 and feared that
he might die, Luther provides topics which everyone,
even powerful princes, might contemplate when facing
suffering.

*On the Papacy in Rome, Against the Most Celebrated
Romanist in Leipzig* (v. 39)
Luther writes in response to Augustine Alveld's
Concerning the Apostolic See, which defends the papacy
as a divine institution. Luther counters with his
assertion that the church is not an institution, but
rather a community of faith and a communion of saints.

A Discussion on How Confession Should Be Made
(v. 39)
Luther asserts that the believer should not come to
confession with a sense of fear, but rather with confi-
dence that God, to whom one confesses, is faithful and
will forgive the sinner as he has promised.

Sermon on the Ban (v. 39)
In this sermon preached in December, 1519, Luther
argues that sin is a lack of trust in God's grace, not the
failure to obey rules established by the church.

The Babylonian Captivity of the Church (v. 36)
In this second of the three famous treatises of 1520,
Luther looks at the sacramental system of the church,
by which the church hierarchy is able to hold the laity
captive to its corrupt system. He discusses each of the

1520
(cont'd.)
seven sacraments, but concentrates on the Lord's Supper. See Chapter 4.

A Treatise on the New Testament, That is, the Holy Mass (v. 35)
Luther no longer sees the Lord's Supper as a sacrifice in this devotional piece written before *The Babylonian Captivity of the Church.* Properly understood, says Luther, "the mass is nothing else than a testament and sacrament in which God makes a pledge to us and gives us grace and mercy."

The Freedoms of a Christian (v. 31)
This is the third of Luther's three famous treatises of 1520. It is a clear statement of Luther's evangelical theology, applied to the life of the Christian. See Chapter 4.

Why the Books of the Pope and His Disciples Were Burned by Doctor Martin Luther (v. 31)
In the middle of October, 1520, the papal bull threatening Luther with excommunication was published at the court of Charles V, accompanied by the burning of Luther's book. On December 10, a group of students at the University of Wittenberg burned copies of the cannon law, papal decretals, and works of scholastic philosophy. Luther tossed the papal bull into the fire.

1521
A Sermon on the Three Kinds of Good Life for the Instruction of Consciences (v. 44)
Luther teaches that God puts into the heart of those who by faith have trusted in Jesus Christ, the desire to do good works, that is, the works God has commanded, not those demanded by men.

An Instruction to Penitents Concerning the Forbidden Books of Dr. M. Luther (v. 44)
Luther seeks to comfort, console, and advise those who have been denied access to the sacraments, because they possessed, or had read, *Luther's Works.*

The Judgment of Martin Luther on Monastic Vows
(v. 44)
Luther argues against the popular belief that the
monastic life is somehow more spiritual than the
Christian's life outside the monastery. He says that the
Christian must live in God's world, not the monastery.

Sermon on the Worthy Reception of the Sacrament
(v. 42)
One week before his historic appearance before the
Diet of Worms in 1521, Luther preached this sermon
in which he states that the sacrament of the Lord's
Supper is meant for those who by faith believe and trust
in Christ's power to heal and restore them.

Comfort When Facing Grave Temptations (v. 42)
Luther writes to Christians facing fear and temptations.
He advises them to remember that they are a part of
the communion of saints, the Body of Christ, and,
armed with the word of God, can look to this invisible
church for comfort when in distress.

To the Goat in Leipzig (v. 39)
The "Leipzig Goat" referred to here is Jerome Emser,
who wrote against the reforms Luther proposed in *To
the Christian Nobility of the German Nation* (1521). It
is the first of four treatises against Emser, all of which
are helpful for understanding Luther's doctrines of the
church and ministry.

Concerning the Answer of the Goat in Leipzig (v. 39)
Luther's response to Jerome Emser's response to *To the
Goat in Leipzig.*

*Answer to the Hyperchristian, Hyperspiritual, and
Hyperlearned Book by Goat Emser in Leipzig—Including
Some Thoughts Regarding His Companion, the Fool
Murner* (v. 39)
This is the most significant of the four treatises Luther
wrote in his debate with Jerome Emser. Once again
Luther presents his arguments for the priesthood of the

1521   believer. Also, Luther asserts the authority of Scripture
(cont'd.) over ecclesiastical tradition.

Dr. Luther's Retraction of the Error Forced Upon Him by the Most Highly Learned Priest of God, Sir Jerome Emser, Vicar in Meissen (v. 39)
Luther again defends his doctrine of the priesthood of the believer, in this fourth and final treatise directed against Jerome Emser.

The Misuse of the Mass (v. 36)
In this followup to *The Babylonian Captivity,* Luther dismisses the Mass, or Lord's Supper, as celebrated in the Roman Catholic church. Luther rejects the idea of it as a sacrifice, and goes on to reject the Roman Catholic concept of priesthood, believing instead that every Christian is his or her own priest. Also, he begins to question whether it is right to hold back the cup of wine from the laity.

A Brief Instruction on What to Look for and Expect in the Gospels (v. 35)
This is one of a series of sermons on the epistles and gospels known as the "Wartburg Postil," since they were written while Luther was in hiding at Frederick the Wise's Wartburg Castle. The message is that there is but one Christ and one gospel in both the Old and New Testaments, and that he is a gift of God, bestowed through the preaching of the word. Thus, when the Scriptures are no longer preached, God abandons the people to the lies of men.

Against Latomus (v. 32)
In this response to a book against Luther by Latomus (Jacobus Masson), Luther presents his ideas on the relationship between sin and grace, law and gospel, and justification and sanctification.

Defense and Explanation of All the Articles (v. 32)
This is one of Luther's four responses to the papal bull, *Exsurge Domine,* which condemned forty-one of Luther's *Ninety-Five Theses* as heretical.

Luther at the Diet of Worms (v. 32)
Although not by Luther himself, two contemporary accounts of Luther's appearance before the Diet of Worms (1521) are included. The first is by a friend and the second is by Aleander (1480–1542), the papal nuncio to the court of Charles V.

The Persons Related by Consanguinity and Affinity who Are Forbidden to Marry According to the Scriptures, Leviticus 18 (v. 45)

The Estate of Marriage (v. 45)
Luther discusses who may and may not marry, the grounds for divorce—he recognizes three—and finding happiness in a Christian marriage.

A Sincere Admonition by Martin Luther to All Christians to Guard Against Insurrection and Rebellion (v. 45)
Luther urges his followers to refrain from rebellion and other acts of violence. God will avenge himself in his own appropriate way.

Personal Prayer Book (v. 43)
A popular devotional work modeled on, and meant to replace, the personal prayer books common during the Middle Ages. Luther uses the Ten Commandments, the Apostles' Creed, and the Lord's Prayer to communicate the basic teachings of the Christian faith in terms that the ordinary layperson could understand.

A Letter to Hans von Rechenberg (v. 43)
Luther seeks to answer the question of whether or not a person who dies without faith can be saved. Luther's answer is that no one can be saved except by faith.

1522 *A Letter of Consolation to All Who Suffer Persecution* (v. 43)
Luther seeks to comfort and encourage Hartmut von Cronberg, a young nobleman who was suffering persecution because of his evangelical faith and support of Luther.

1522   *Against the Spiritual Estate of the Pope and the Bishops,*
(cont'd.) *Falsely So Called* (v. 39)
          Luther rejects the doctrine of "holy orders" and argues
          for the right of priests to marry.

          Receiving Both Kinds in the Sacrament (v. 36)
          Luther continues his discussion of the Lord's Supper
          from *The Babylonian Captivity* and *The Misuse of the
          Mass.* Here he concentrates on whether one or both of
          the elements (bread and wine) should be used in the
          Mass. He believes that consideration must be given to
          the spiritual maturity of the people, and thus reform of
          the Mass must be undertaken.

          Avoiding the Doctrines of Men, and *A Reply to the Texts
          Cited in Defense of the Doctrines of Men* (v. 35)
          Luther directs his remarks to those (e.g., monks) who
          had taken vows on food and other matters of lifestyle.
          He asserts that the Bible alone is the final authority in
          matters of lifestyle. The second piece is a response to
          Henry VIII's *Defense of the Seven Sacraments,* written in
          response to Luther's *The Babylonian Captivity of the
          Church.*

1523   *Ordinance of a Common Chest,* and *Fraternal
          Agreement on the Common Chest of the Entire Assembly
          at Leising* (v. 45)
          Luther tries to provide guidance on how parish finances
          might be reorganized so as to provide support for the
          parish, as well as the poor and destitute of the parish.
          Luther includes the ordinance drawn up by the parish
          of Leising in 1523.

          That Jesus Christ Was Born a Jew (v. 45)
          Luther gives his response to the rumor that he taught
          that "Jesus was conceived of the seed of Joseph, and
          that Mary was not a virgin, but had many sons after
          Christ." He then goes on to urge Christians to stop
          discriminating against Jews and treat them with
          Christian love, so as to win them to Christ.
          See Chapter 6.

The Adoration of the Sacrament (v. 36)
Luther discusses what should be the attitude of the
believer towards the elements in the Lord's Supper. He
also makes a distinction (based upon his study of
1 Cor. 10:16, 17) between the body of Christ as the
spiritual union of all believers, and the body of Christ
which is distributed in the bread and wine of the Lord's
Supper. Luther insisted that all who come to the Lord's
Communion table, both worthy and unworthy, receive
the Lord's body.

*That a Christian Assembly or Congregation Has the
Right and Power to Judge All Teaching and to Call,
Appoint, and Dismiss Teachers, Established and Proven
by Scripture* (v. 39)
Luther defends the right of a congregation to call and
to ordain ministers.

Concerning the Ministry (v. 40)
In this treatise addressed to the followers of Jan Hus in
Bohemia, Luther defends the right of a congregation to
elect its own ministers.

To All Christians in Worms (v. 43)
Luther seeks to encourage evangelical Christians in
Worms, where he made his famous "Here I Stand"
speech. No doubt news of the first Lutheran martyrs,
who were burned at the stake in Brussels on July 1,
1523, was in the back of his mind.

Temporal Authority: To What Extent it Should be Obeyed
(v. 45)
Believing that Matthew 5:38–41 teaches that Christians
are forbidden to resist evil, Luther goes on to argue
that they may engage in passive disobedience, when
they are being coerced in matters of faith by the secular
authorities.

*An Exhortation to the Knights of the Teutonic Order that
They Lay Aside False Chastity and Assume the True
Chastity of Wedlock* (v. 45)

1524   *Trade and Usury* (v. 45)
Luther's lack of knowledge of capitalism, which was
beginning to appear in Germany at the beginning of
the sixteenth century, is evident in this treatise on
economics. Luther's view of economics is that of
Aristotle and the scholastic theologians. Luther did not
believe that money produced wealth. For him, money
was merely a means of providing subsistence helping
the poor.

*Exposition of Psalm 127, for the Christians at Riga in
Livonia* (v. 45)
This piece was composed for, and dedicated to, the
Lutherans in Riga on the Baltic Sea. Since Luther was
particularly concerned at the time with the financing of
Christian schools, etc., he comments on the proper
attitude of Christians towards material goods.

*To the Councilmen of All Cities in Germany, That They
Establish and Maintain Christian Schools* (v. 45)
Luther expresses his firm belief in Christian education,
and calls upon the secular authorities to establish
Christian schools throughout Germany. It is in such
schools that they will receive the spiritual and practical
education that will make them good citizens.

*A Christian Letter of Consolation to the People of
Mittenberg* (v. 43)
The people of Mittenberg accepted the new evangelical
faith, but were then forced back into the Roman
Catholic church. Luther writes to them saying that they
should rejoice in their suffering for the gospel's sake,
and pray for preachers who will proclaim the true faith.

*Letter to the Christians at Strassburg in Opposition to the
Fanatic Spirit* (v. 40)
Luther warns the brethren in Strassburg against the
false teachings of his former colleague, Andreas
Carlstadt.

Letter to the Princes of Saxony Concerning the Rebellious Spirit (v. 40)
Fearing that the radical preaching of Thomas Müntzer would lead to civil unrest and rebellion, Luther writes to the Saxon princes, reminding them that it is their duty to maintain order. He calls upon the princes to take action against Müntzer and his followers, before it is too late.

That Parents Should Neither Compel nor Hinder the Marriage of Their Children, and *That Children Should Not Become Engaged Without Their Parents' Consent* (v. 45)

1525   *The Burning of Brother Henry* (v. 32)
Luther attempts to comfort the Christians in Bremen, whose pastor, Henry of Zutphen, was martyred on December 4, 1524.

How Christians Should Regard Moses (v. 35)
Luther deals here with the problem of the relationship between the Old Testament and the New Testament and the relationship between the Old Testament law (i.e., the Mosaic law) and the gospel. Luther asserts that Christians are not bound by the Old Testament law where it disagrees with the New Testament or "the law implanted within all men by nature."

The Abomination of the Secret Mass (v. 36)
In this treatise, Luther again stresses what he asserted earlier in 1521, in *The Misuse of the Mass,* that is, that the mass is not a sacrifice, and therefore masses for the dead and private masses should be discontinued.

Against the Heavenly Prophets in the Matter of Images and Sacraments (v. 40)
Luther directed this harshly worded treatise at Andreas Carlstadt and the other "spiritualists." In it Luther defends the authority of Scripture against the mysticism that Luther felt underlay Carlstadt's teachings.

1525 *Admonition to Peace, A Reply to the Twelve Articles of*
(cont'd.) *the Peasants in Swabia* (v. 46)
This is Luther's response to the Twelve Articles, or demands, made by the peasants on the eve of the Peasants' Revolt of 1525. Luther tries to encourage the peasants to avoid violence and seek justice through peaceful means. See Chapter 6.

Against the Robbing and Murdering Hordes of Peasants (v. 46)
The Peasants's Revolt began before Luther's *Admonition to Peace* was published. In this very harshly worded polemic, which appeared at the height of the revolt, Luther calls upon the princes to suppress the revolt and punish the peasants. See Chapter 6.

An Open Letter on the Harsh Book Against the Peasants (v. 46)
Luther was widely criticized, even by his friends, for the harsh and vicious attack upon the peasants in *Against the Robbing and Murdering Hordes of Peasants.* In this response to that criticism, Luther make no apologies, but condemns those who dare to criticize or seek to correct him. See Chapter 6.

1526 *The Bondage of the Will* (v. 33)
In the debate over freedom of the will with Erasmus of Rotterdam, Luther weighed in with this defense of his position that the individual's will is totally captive to sin. There is nothing that the individual may do that might contribute to his or her salvation. See Chapter 5.

The Sacrament of the Body and Blood of Christ—Against the Fanatics (v. 36)
This is the published version of several sermons in which Luther tried to distinguish his position on the Lord's Supper from that of the South German and Swiss reformers (e.g., Huldrich Zwingli), whom Luther felt were too radical.

Whether Soldiers, Too, Can be Saved (v. 46)
Luther asserts that being a soldier is an honorable

profession, since the use of arms in defense is a God-given duty of the state.

An Answer to Several Questions on Monastic Vows (v. 46)

1527   *That These Words of Christ, "This is My Body," Still Stand Firm Against the Fanatics* (v. 37)
Luther responds to some two dozen treatises published between 1524 and 1527 that attacked his views on the Lord's Supper. This together with *Confession Concerning Christ's Supper* (1528) constitutes Luther's most comprehensive discussion of the Lord's Supper.

A Letter of Consolation to the Christians at Halle (v. 43)
Luther writes words of consolation to the congregation of an evangelical believer in Halle, who was murdered, apparently for his Christian faith.

Whether One May Flee from a Deadly Plague (v. 43)
When the plague struck Breslau in Silesia, the clergy there asked Luther if it was right for the clergy to flee from the plague. In this response, Luther answers in the negative. Neither, clergy, nor any official, has the right before God to flee in order to save his own life. Rather, they are bound to remain and serve their flock. When the plague struck Wittenberg in August, 1527, Luther refused to leave the city, despite orders from his prince to do so.

1528   *Instructions for the Visitors of Parish Pastors in Electoral Saxony* (v. 40)
Originally written by Philip Melanchthon and later revised by Luther, these are Luther's instructions to Elector John of Saxony on the organization and support of the churches in the wake of the overthrow of the authority of the Catholic bishops.

Concerning Rebaptism (v. 40)
Luther defends infant baptism in this treatise against the Anabaptists and their advocacy of believer's baptism.

1528   *Confession Concerning Christ's Supper* (v. 37)
(cont'd.) Luther's final and most comprehensive published
              discussion of the Lord's Supper. It became the
              authoritative word on the subject for Lutherans.

1529   *On War Against the Turk* (v. 46)
              Luther asserts that a war against the Turks (Muslims)
              must not be a crusade. Scripture does not give the
              church any right to lead a war of any kind. The defense
              of the realm and its subjects is a duty assigned by God
              to the secular authority, not the church.

              The Marburg Colloquy and the Marburg Articles
              (v. 38)
              The Marburg Colloquy was arranged by Philip of
              Hesse with hopes of bringing unity to the Protestant
              Reformation by finding agreement between Luther and
              the Swiss reformers, Huldrich Zwingli and John
              Oecolampadius. This is the published version of the
              dialogue between the participants, and the *Articles* that
              came out of the colloquy.

1530   *On Marriage Matters* (v. 46)
              Luther provides guidance from Scripture on matters
              that were previously covered under canon law.

              A Sermon on Keeping Children in School (v. 46)
              Once again Luther urges parents to give their children
              an education, so that they can serve God in the church
              and be good citizens.

              Exhortation to All Clergy Assembled at Augsburg, 1530
              (v. 34)
              Luther spent the period of the Diet of Augsburg
              (1530) safely in residence at the nearby castle of
              Coburg. During that time, he drafted this exhortation,
              a summary of all his teachings up to that time.
              Sometimes called "Luther's Augsburg Confession," it
              summarizes all the reforms and changes brought about
              by the Reformation up to 1530.

Sayings in Which Luther Found Comfort (v. 43)
Luther is supposed to have had a habit of writing Bible verses or comforting thoughts on the walls where he could readily see them. This is a collection of Bible verses and comments by Luther from the period when he was staying at Coburg Castle during the Diet of Augsburg in 1530. They were taken down and published by Matthaeus Flaccius (1520–75), a professor of Hebrew at the University of Wittenberg.

That a Christian Should Bear His Cross with Patience (v. 43)
These are the notes for, or based upon, a sermon preached by Luther to a group of theologians on their way to the Diet of Augsburg in 1530. Luther met with them at Coburg Castle and tried to encourage them. His theme is that the Christian should welcome suffering, if it is truly for Christ's sake that one is suffering.

On Translating: An Open Letter (v. 35)
Luther defends his controversial rendering of Romans 3:28, to which he added the word, "alone." Luther argues that the added word was linguistically and theologically necessary.

Admonition Concerning the Sacrament of the Body and Blood of Our Lord (v. 38)
In this devotional piece published one year after the Marburg Colloquy, Luther deals with the place of the sacrament of the Lord's Supper in the life of the church. In the sacrament, the believers share in the gift of Christ's body and blood, and remember his death on the cross. Participation leads to greater faith in God, love for one's neighbors, and patient bearing of affliction and suffering.

The Keys (v. 40)
Luther defends the biblical doctrine of salvation by faith alone against the medieval church's teaching that the power of the keys to open or shut the doors of

1530   heaven belong to the church by right of succession
(cont'd.) from St. Peter.

1531   *Commentary on the Alleged Imperial Edict, 1531*
          (v. 34)
          Luther defends the teaching of Scripture in this
          refutation of the imperial edict of 1531, giving the
          Protestants until April 15, 1531 to submit to the
          Catholic church and imperial authorities. Luther
          discusses such topics as "the mass, free will, justification
          by faith, prebends [stipends], marriage of the clergy,
          penance, the examination of preachers by ordinances,
          holy days, forbidden foods, and the vows of monks and
          nuns."

          *Dr. Martin Luther's Warning to His Dear German
          People* (v. 47)
          Luther writes urging the German princes to resist, by
          passive or armed means, any effort by Charles V after
          the Diet of Augsburg (1530) to forcibly return the
          Protestants to the Roman Catholic church.

          Defense of the Translation of the Psalms (v. 35)
          Luther discusses problems encountered in translating
          the Old Testament. He insists that the translator must
          consider the "sense," as well as the words, when
          translating the Hebrew original into a foreign language,
          e.g, German.

1532   *Infiltrating and Clandestine Preachers* (v. 40)
          Luther is writing against the Anabaptist preachers, who
          have not been called to preach by the proper
          authorities. He urges the secular authorities to be on
          the alert for them. This piece illustrates how even for
          Luther, there is no place for religious freedom or
          toleration.

1533   *The Private Mass and the Consecration of Priests*
          (v. 38)
          Luther attacks the then prevalent Roman Catholic
          practice of private Masses, wherein the priest celebrated

the Mass by himself. Luther questions whether the gift of the body and blood of Jesus Christ is present in a private Mass, since no believer is present, and hence no real communion of persons. Luther also attacks the related practice of consecrating individuals as priests for the sole purpose of celebrating private Masses.

1534   *A Letter of Dr. Martin Luther Concerning His Book on the Private Mass* (v. 38)
Luther seeks to refute the charge that he taught a purely symbolic view of the Lord's Supper by affirming his belief in the real presence of the body and blood of Jesus Christ in the Lord's Supper.

1535   *Theses Concerning Faith and Law* (v. 34)
Luther chooses to deal with the doctrine of justification by faith in, "The Theses for the Doctoral Examination of Hieronymus Weller and Nikolaus Medler." Included are "The Doctoral Examination of Hieronymus Weller and Nikolaus Medler," and "The Graduation Address Presented by Hieronymus Weller," also written by Luther.

A Simple Way to Pray (43)
Dedicated to Peter Beskendorf, Luther's barber, this is Luther's outline for personal devotions which he, himself, used and recommended for anyone wishing to develop a program of personal devotions.

1536   *The Disputation Concerning Man* (v. 34)
Luther continues the theme of justification by faith in this disputation from January 14, 1536. He praises reason, but asserts that whether in theology or philosophy, reason cannot answer the question of "what is man?"

The Disputation Concerning Justification (v. 34)
This disputation from October 10, 1536, shows that Luther's views on the doctrine of justification by faith in 1536 are identical to his views expressed in his lectures on Romans between November 1515 and September 1516.

1538   *Against the Sabbatarians: Letter to a Good Friend*
(v. 47)
Luther blames the rise of Sabbatarianism (the
observance of Saturday as the Lord's day and other Old
Testament Jewish practices) on the influence of the
Jews.

The Three Symbols or Creeds of the Christian Faith
(v. 34)
Luther is concerned with the mystery of the Trinity and
the person and works of Jesus Christ in this exposition
of the three oldest creeds of the Christian church—the
Apostles' Creed, the Athanasian Creed, and the *Te
Deum laudamus,* or so-called Ambrosian hymn. He
concludes by citing the Nicene Creed.

*Counsel of a Committee of Several Cardinals with
Luther's Preface* (v. 34)
A commission of nine cardinals drafted a memorandum
to serve as a platform for reform of the Roman
Catholic church by general council. Pope Paul III
called for such a council to meet in Mantua (later
changed to Trent). Luther published the memorandum
together with his response in which he ridiculed the
memorandum as an attempt to cover up the church's
failure to reform itself.

Preface to Galeatius Capella's History (v. 34)
This is Luther's preface to Galeatius Capella's history of
the reign of Francesco II Sforza, duke of Milan. Luther
was a lover of history. He expressed the belief that
everyone should be aware of their history, because God
is always at work in history.

1539   *Preface to the Wittenberg Edition of Luther's German
Writings* (v. 34)
Luther expresses his fear that Christians will forsake the
reading of Scripture for the reading of Christian books,
such as those he wrote. He says that he would rather all
of his books perish, and Christians read the Bible
instead. The only value his own books serve, he says, is
as a historical record of his struggle against the papacy.

The Disputation Concerning the Passage: "The Word Was Made Flesh" (John 1:14) (v.38)
Luther seeks to ground his firm belief in the real presence of Christ's body and blood in the sacrament of the Lord's Supper in the incarnation. Luther is in agreement with the early church Fathers, when he asserts that God takes on human form in the incarnation. Jesus Christ, the Second Person of the Trinity, became a human being without surrendering his divinity. Human beings do not become divine in any sense.

On the Councils and the Church (v. 41)
From his study of the early church Fathers and the great ecumenical councils (beginning with the Jerusalem Council recorded in Acts 15), Luther concludes that the church must be based upon Scripture. He writes: "Now, wherever you hear or see this word preached, believed, professed, and lived, do not doubt that the true *ecclesia sancta catholica,* 'a Christian holy people' must be there, even though their number is small."

Against the Antinomians (v. 47)
Luther addresses the ongoing controversy over the relationship between the Old Testament law that brings one to repentance and the gospel that brings redemption. Luther seeks to demonstrate that salvation by grace through faith does not give one a license for moral laxity. Pastors must go on preaching on the law, as well as salvation.

1541   *Against Hanswurst* (v. 41)
Luther asserts that the church of the Reformation is not a new church, but the true church which is always present on earth.

Appeal for Prayer Against the Turks (v. 43)
The Turks (Muslims) under Suleiman the Great are threatening to invade Germany. Luther sees God's hand in these events. He urges Christians to go into

1541   battle acknowledging that they, too, are sinners
(cont'd.) deserving God's judgment. If Christians turn back to
         God with repentant hearts, perhaps he will hear them
         and grant them more than they deserve.

1542   *The Licentiate Examination of Heinrich Schmedenstede*
         (v. 34)
         Luther uses Hebrews 13:8 as the basis for his remarks
         relating the doctrine of justification of faith alone to the
         question of how people were saved before Jesus Christ,
         since Jesus Christ alone is the way, the truth, and the
         light.

         Luther's Will (v. 34)

         Comfort for Women who Have Had a Miscarriage
         (v. 43)
         Luther attempts to provide comfort for mothers whose
         children died before they were baptized. It is aimed at
         the grieving mother, not the philosopher or theologian.

1543   *On the Jews and Their Lies* (v. 47)
         Here in his most controversial treatise, Luther calls for
         the princes to institute harsh policies towards the Jews.
         See Chapter 6.

1544   *Brief Confession Concerning the Holy Sacrament*
         (v. 38)
         This is Luther's brief, final affirmation of the real
         presence of Christ's body and blood in the Lord's
         Supper. It demonstrates that there is no difference
         between the "Young Luther" and the "Old Luther"
         with respect to his theology of the cross.

1545   *Preface to the Complete Edition of Luther's Latin
         Writings* (v. 34)
         In this Preface, Luther provides a valuable summary of
         the early Reformation and his road from monk to
         reformer. It is an important historical document.

Against the Thirty-two Articles of the Louvain Theologists
(v. 34)
Luther responds to the theses composed by the faculty
of Louvain University at the request of Charles V. They
were meant to serve as a kind of Roman Catholic
confession of faith, and were sent by the emperor to
religious teachers and church leaders. The "Thirty-two
Theses" of the Louvain theologians, together with the
emperor's confirmation letter, precedes Luther's
seventy-five counter theses.

Against the Roman Papacy, an Institution of the Devil
(v. 41)
Luther holds forth no hope for the reformation of the
Roman Catholic church in this attack on the corrupt
Renaissance papacy, which Luther sees as a demonic
institution and the Antichrist attacking God's authority
on earth, both secular and spiritual.

To the Saxon Princes (v. 43)
Luther advises the princes not to release Duke Henry
the Younger of Braunschweig, an implacable foe of the
Reformation, from captivity. He also advises the duke
to renounce his title and repent, if he wishes to save his
soul.

Bibliographical Note

The individual wishing to look further into the subject of Martin Luther is likely to be overwhelmed by the vast quantity of sources available. A quick search on the Internet reveals approximately 1,900 Web sites that offer varying degrees of information, for example, biographies, time lines, popular and scholarly articles, excerpts from Luther's works, etc. The beginner would probably do well to begin with a video or two, then read a good basic biography, and finally turn to books on areas of special interest.

The classic motion picture, *Martin Luther* (105 minutes), nominated for two academy awards in 1953, is available as a Vision Video from Gateway Films. It is based on Roland Bainton's classic biography, *Here I Stand: A Life of Martin Luther* (Nashville: Abingdon Press, 1950). Another good starting point is the thirty-minute documentary, *Where Luther Walked,* also a Vision Video from Gateway Films. It is a walk through the historic sites associated with Martin Luther's life, narrated by Roland Bainton. There are two recent drama productions, *Martin Luther: Heretic* (BBC, seventy minutes), available from Family Films, and *Martin Luther: Reluctant Revolutionary* (PBS, 120 minutes), available from PBS. Finally, there is the recent motion picture, *Luther* (2003). A widely acclaimed German production, it stars Joseph Fiennes as Luther and Peter Ustinov as Frederick the Wise.

The quantity of printed sources available is even more daunting than the Internet Web sites. For the beginner, there are a few biographies that may serve as a starting point. Bibliographies and footnotes in these can provide useful guides to further, more specialized studies.

For biographies of Luther, the place to begin is, of course, Roland Bainton's *Here I Stand.* Although many Luther biographies have appeared since its first appearance in 1950, none have surpassed it as a basic introduction to the life and times of Martin Luther. Until his death in 1984, Bainton was the acknowledged dean of Reformation studies. His numerous books on the Reformation and its leaders are very readable and readily available in well-stocked libraries.

Two recent general biographies written especially for the non-specialist are *Martin Luther: A Penguin Life* by Martin E. Marty (New York: Penguin Books, 2004), and *Luther the Reformer: The Story of the Man and His Career* (Minneapolis: Fortress Press, 1986). Other brief, general biographies are Kathleen Benson's *A Man Called Martin Luther* (St. Louis: Concordia Publishing House, 1980); *Martin Luther: An Introduction to His Life and Work*, by Bernhard Lohse and translated by Robert C. Schultz (Philadelphia: Fortress Press, 1986); *Luther: His Life and Times* (New York: Harcourt Brace Jovanovich, 1967); and *Luther Alive: Martin Luther and the Making of the Reformation* (London: Hodder and Stoughton, 1968).

Heiko A. Oberman's *Luther: Man Between God and the Devil*, translated by Eileen Walliser-Schwarzbart (New Haven: Yale University Press, 1990) is a must read for the serious student, but requires a basic knowledge of Luther's life. A recent postmodern interpretation of Luther is Richard Marius's *Martin Luther: The Christian Between God and Death* (Cambridge: Harvard University Press, 1999). Heiko A. Oberman's review of Marius's biography in *The Historian* (Summer, 2000 [available on the Internet at http://www.findarticles.com] should be read along with the book. Finally, the energetic reader may wish to read *The Triumph of Truth: A Life of Martin Luther* (Greenville, SC: Bob Jones University Press, 1996) by the nineteenth-century church historian, J. H. Merle D'Aubigne. Its language is dated, but D'Aubigne's biography of Luther, like his four-volume *History of the Reformation of the Sixteenth Century*, One-Volume Edition (Grand Rapids: Baker Book House, 1986) contains interesting details not found anywhere else.

The reader who wishes to read some of Luther's own works should consult the annotated list of those included in the "official" English language translation, *Luther's Works*, edited by Jaroslav Pelikan and Helmut T. Lehman, 55 volumes (St. Louis: Concordia House; Philadelphia: Fortress Press, 1955–86). *Luther's Works* is now available on CD-ROM from Fortress Press. Various of the more important and popular works are available in single-volume format, hardcover or paperback, and in one-volume collections of excerpts, or complete treatises. Three popular collections are *Martin Luther: Selections from His Writings*, edited by John Dillenberger (New York: Doubleday, 1972), *Martin Luther's Basic Theological Writings*, edited by Timothy F. Lull (Philadelphia: Fortress Press, 1991), and *Three Treatises*, edited by Charles Michael Jacobs (Philadelphia: Fortress Press, 1990).

Index

Martin Luther: A Brief Introduction to His Life and Works
Developmental editor: Andrew J. Davidson
Copy editor/Production editor/Book design: Lucy Herz
Proofreader: Claudia Siler
Cartographer: Jason Casanova, Pegleg Graphics
Printer: McNaughton & Gunn, Inc.